Red Pockets

Red Pockets

Red Pockets

An Offering

ALICE MAH

ALLEN LANE
an imprint of
PENGUIN BOOKS

ALLEN LANE

UK | USA | Canada | Ireland | Australia
India | New Zealand | South Africa

Allen Lane is part of the Penguin Random House group of companies
whose addresses can be found at global.penguinrandomhouse.com.

First published in Great Britain by Allen Lane 2025

001

Printed and bound in Great Britain by Clays Ltd, Elcograf S.p.A.

The authorized representative in the EEA is Penguin Random House Ireland,
Morrison Chambers, 32 Nassau Street, Dublin DO2 YH68

A CIP catalogue record for this book is available from the British Library

978–0–241–60831–9

Penguin Random House is committed to a sustainable future
for our business, our readers and our planet. This book is made from
Forest Stewardship Council® certified paper.

Penguin Random House is committed to a
sustainable future for our business, our readers
and our planet. This book is made from Forest
Stewardship Council® certified paper.

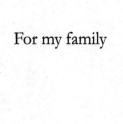

For my family

Contents

PART 3

Burnt Offerings

Prologue

'Are you going to sweep the tombs?' my dad asked me. He rarely mentioned anything about China, and his question took me by surprise.

'Why would I do that?' I had never heard about tomb-sweeping.

'Because that's what you are supposed to do when you go back to the village. You sweep the tombs of your ancestors.' He said this with such a casual air of authority that I couldn't tell if he was serious or not.

Really? Why hadn't he mentioned this before?

It was the summer of 2017, one of the worst wildfire seasons on record in British Columbia, although worse years were yet to come, and I was visiting my parents on Vancouver Island. I planned to go to China the following spring to research toxic polluted cities. I had always wanted to go and finally found the opportunity through my work, as part of a sociological research project on the global petrochemical industry and environmental justice.[1] This would be my second trip to China. My first was a short visit to Beijing in 2015 at the beginning of the project, though I did not manage to see much. This time, I wanted to search for our ancestral clan village in the south.

'You know, your cousin Amanda went to China earlier this year, and she claims that she found the village,' my dad added. 'I don't know if she swept the tombs, though.'

I pressed for more, but that was all he would say. My dad had no interest in visiting China. As a thick ash cloud began to settle over the town, we stayed inside drinking weak coffee.

In retrospect, I probably should have attached more significance to my dad's question.

In 1924, my great-grandmother Woo Doke Yee developed a malignant growth in her neck and inner ear that would not respond to treatment. She wanted to go back to China to see her ageing mother and introduce her to the children. The next year, my great-grandfather Mah Gee Su arranged for the family to make the long journey from the railway town of Cranbrook in British Columbia back to their village in South China. My grandfather Mah Yue Gee wrote about this journey in his unpublished *Memoirs of a Chinese Canadian*.[2] His childhood recollections of the voyage were punctuated by his mother's illness. When they arrived in Vancouver to await the steamship to Hong Kong, they were refused admission to the Hotel Vancouver because they were not 'High Class' Chinese merchants or diplomats. Through clan networks, my great-grandfather managed to find a large house where they could stay in the Shaughnessy Heights area, named after the first president of the Canadian Pacific Railway, with servants to care for his ailing wife. Aboard the steamship, nurses attended to her, and the family stopped at a hospital in Hong Kong before carrying on to Canton (Guangzhou).

They took a rickety train to their clan village of South Uplands and were met by relatives with sedan chairs, who carried them along the muddy path through the flooded rice fields to their family home. Shortly after arriving, my great-grandmother died in her sleep. My grandfather recalled that 'we three children were somewhat elated that Mother had gone peacefully to heaven after such a long period of painful illness'.[3] They had received Christian teachings in Gim Shan (Gold Mountain),[4] the overseas Chinese name for North America, named after the promised land of the Gold Rush, that heaven was a reward for death.

My great-grandmother was given both a Christian and a Buddhist funeral, with a Christian minister from Canton and a Buddhist priest from the local temple to honour the ancestors. Clan relatives came to the burial ceremony all dressed in white, weeping and wailing, as was customary in Chinese burial rites.[5] My grandfather wrote somewhat ruefully that he and his brother and sister were not able to cry at their mother's funeral, and for years afterwards, they were known as 'the barbaric foreign-devil Mah children who would not grieve at their mother's funeral'.[6]

I have a strange affinity with those foreign-devil Mah children. I was one of four Mah children who grew up in a majority white Christian town in Canada on the unceded land of the Indigenous Wet'suwet'en people. We had no religion. Close in age, with long dark hair, we were often mistaken by the townspeople for one another, and for members of the Wet'suwet'en. When I was in high school, a local boy once asked me where I 'really' came from. He could trace his family history to the Netherlands and was a member of the Dutch Reformed Church, the dominant church in our town. When I responded that my dad was Chinese and my mom was white, he said, 'So you have no home then.' I recognized the ignorance in this comment, but still, it got under my skin. Wasn't our town my home?

Twenty years later, after living and working in many different cities, from Vancouver, Montreal and Ottawa, to London, Oxford and Berlin, to Coventry, where I had stayed the longest, I returned to my grandfather's ancestral rice village in China.

It was a homecoming of sorts, an unsettling kind, showing up nearly a century too late. I did not expect to be confronted so startlingly with my own rootlessness. I did not heed my dad's warning, either. I failed to sweep the tombs. At the time, it did not seem so important.

Since that journey, I have been haunted by my ancestors' neglected graves. In Chinese folk religious beliefs, ancestors who are abandoned by their descendants become hungry ghosts, unleashing illnesses, misfortunes and crop failures.[7] The Buddhist figure of the hungry ghost inhabits one of the lower realms of hell, akin to purgatory, and suffers from endless cravings. Ancient Buddhist texts describe thirty-six types of hungry ghost, such as the Burning-Mouth ghost, whose food bursts into flames when it touches their lips; the Needle-Mouth ghost, who can only eat tiny amounts of food through a mouth the size of the eye of a needle; and the

Vomit-Eaters, Excrement-Eaters and Spittle-Eaters, who are forced to subsist on repulsive substances.[8]

I have felt the anguish of hungry ghosts in our fractured times, unmoored feelings of grief and despair shared across cultures, generations and species. Ecological collapse, life out of balance, hungry ghosts: it is difficult to deny, whatever we call it, but almost impossible to face. Slowly, I am beginning to recognize the debts that I owe and the impossibility of returning to past worlds. Some obligations have been lost in time and translation, but others endure and cry out to be honoured. As pollution exceeds safe planetary limits, rare moths, ground-nesting birds and countless other species die out, and communities around the world face deadly wildfires and floods, I have come to understand that these obligations are both material and spiritual, a fragile balance of give and take. So, I set out in search of an acceptable offering, imperfect though it may be.

PART ONE

Qingming

1. Western Peaceful Place

'Ah,' Amanda said, smiling out of the car window as we passed flooded rice fields and soft green mountains. 'We are coming home.'

I looked out at the banana trees tied together along the edge of the dusty road to protect them against the monsoon season. Home? Nothing could feel further from home.

I was filled with all the anticipation of a first visit, but I should have known better. My cousin Amanda had made the first only months before, breaking a ninety-year spell of clan separation since our grandfather's last visit. Once she had found our ancestral village, there was no going back.

Our grandfather Mah Yue Gee (Henry was his English name) described this rural landscape in his memoirs and recounted catching malaria during his stay in the village as a child. Yet somehow, I hadn't imagined such a tropical place. This was more how I pictured Vietnam, from films about the war. Even the mountains of Taishan (Exalted Hills),[1] the region where our village was located, were nothing like the sloping mountains of my hometown in northern British Columbia (BC). The Exalted Hills were short and covered in shrubby trees.

We followed the road past miles of rice paddies, their

new green shoots glinting in the sun. We passed villages with faded brick and stone buildings, resembling British and Spanish architecture from previous centuries. Farmers appeared in the water scattering rice shoots by hand. Narrow roads jutted across the rice fields from the main road into the villages, each with its own arched gateway inscribed with Chinese characters. At last, we turned onto one such road, towards the gateway of South Uplands.

'This is like the downtown of our village,' Amanda said, in tour guide mode. 'It looks different when it's not raining.'

'I hope there will be less mosquitoes this time,' said Lily, our driver and translator, who had accompanied Amanda on the first trip. This time the car was full, with Amanda's husband Matt, my research assistant Ying and me sitting in the back.

The tension that was simmering throughout the day eased. We were arriving late, but we were here.

We met up the evening before our trip at a hotel in the old town in Guangzhou. Ying and I were researching petrochemical areas on the outskirts of the city, and Amanda and Matt were travelling. The plan was to leave from the hotel early the next morning, following our grandfather's journey of 1925, from Canton through Sun Ning Sang, the regional capital of Taishan, where his family would have taken the local train to the Mah village. Each of us carried different expectations of the trip.

When I had first emailed Amanda, all I wanted to know was the village's location. She replied that it would be easier for her to come to China and show me in person.

'There's plenty to see in the village,' Amanda told me. 'It's almost just as Grandpa described it. Of course, some things have been destroyed, like the interiors of the clan halls. But the people and the mountains are still there. And they remember and have stories about our great-grandmother, great-grandfather and his second wife.'

In 1901, our great-grandfather Mah Gee Su built a joint house in the new subdivision called Western Peaceful Place in their clan village with his brother Mah Gee Sing. According to our grandfather, the original subdivision included 'about ten houses in two rows all alike with the entrances facing each other across a paved stone laneway', all for overseas or Hong Kong families.[2] After making money during the BC Gold Rush and the railway boom in Canada, our great-grandfather returned to the village to start a family. The matchmakers found him a bride from a small clan in Taishan, our great-grandmother Woo Doke Yee, who could write letters and would accept an overseas husband. In 1914, our great-grandfather arranged for his wife and first daughter to join him in Cranbrook, BC, where his business, Hep Chong General Merchants, in Chinatown was flourishing.

'So, you said Uncle is back home, or is he playing mahjong?' Amanda asked Lily. In fact, we had no real uncle in the village. The village elder who had direct memories of our family's history had become, for Amanda, our Uncle Mah. We had no other connections, although nearly everyone in the village, of course, was a Mah.

11

'He's playing mahjong over on that side now.' Lily waved off into the distance. 'Remember, this is also your house,' she added, pointing to a dilapidated two-storey white brick building with arched colonnades on the balconies. 'The bricks are from your house.'

Amanda had already told me about the house over a drink in the empty hotel bar the night before. Our ancestral house had been expropriated during the Cultural Revolution in the late 1960s, when many overseas families were deemed 'disloyal Nationalists', and the bricks had been used to make a new clan hall.

We continued along the road past more banana trees and then turned left into Western Peaceful Place. At the entrance, opposite a modern red and white brick house, there was a small grove of trees with thick surface roots, each surrounded by concrete benches.

'That's kind of the main gathering junction point,' Amanda said. 'If they weren't all in mahjong right now, they'd be sitting out on that corner.' We were expecting to meet the clan at the gathering place upon our arrival, but nobody was there, so we kept driving. Lily's phone rang, attached to the dashboard of her car. She tapped to answer. It was Uncle Mah. His voice was full of animated rising tones, and she responded with soft lilting tones. They were speaking Taishanese, the language of Chinatowns across North America, a dialect of the Yue branch of Chinese. It was familiar sounding, so unlike the Mandarin that I had been trying to learn. Uncle Mah was at home now, and he was waiting for us.

As we continued along the road, the buildings became more regular, aligned in rows. An elderly man stood in the middle of the road hanging clothes on a washing line, and chickens strutted about. The afternoon sun cast a pleasant glow.

'And this is the pond,' Amanda announced. We all looked to our left at the calm green water by the side of the road, with more brick houses beyond it. As a child, our grandfather had helped to harvest the pond, standing barefoot in the muddy bottom to catch the catfish and eels, which burrowed in the mud to escape.

I found it difficult to hear my own thoughts with the running commentary, and yet I was grateful to have a guide. If I had come on my own, I wouldn't have come this far. I would have been happy just to find the main village gateway and stop for a few moments to take in the view of the rice fields and the Exalted Hills.

'This, to the left, is Uncle Mah's new house,' Amanda said as the road opened out onto a square, gesturing towards a building that resembled the one at the junction. 'It's his new house with modern amenities that his children built for him. But they prefer to live in the old house.'

With that, Lily turned off the engine, and we stepped out towards the original houses of Western Peaceful Place, where Uncle Mah lived with his wife. Amanda supposed we should call her Auntie. Married women in China traditionally keep their surnames, but we never asked Auntie hers. Of all the people we were to meet in the village, she was the one who showed us the gentle kindness of an Auntie, an understanding of what we might be looking for. Uncle Mah had another agenda.

As the car doors opened, I fumbled in the bag full of gifts at my feet. I'd brought a dozen mini-tins of English tea shaped like Big Ben and British telephone boxes, and three Scottie dog shortbread tins.

'You should be aware of the cultural expectation that we arrive with gifts for the clan,' Amanda advised me prior to our trip. Gifts from your home country were especially welcome.

'Should I bring all of the gifts?' I asked Ying, who was gathering her own bag with sweets from Macau.

'Why not?' Ying said. 'What else are you going to do with them?' We had carefully portioned out gifts for the people we planned to meet during the rest of our journey in China, and we wanted to travel light.

We followed Amanda into a lane between two dark grey brick houses. If it was just the four of us, Amanda had said, we could ask to stay at Uncle Mah's house. I made the case for the hotel.

Uncle Mah and Auntie welcomed us inside, and Auntie set about making the tea. This felt strangely familiar, reminding me of trips to Toronto as a child when we met my dad's relatives. At eighty-six, Uncle Mah was the oldest man in the village, with watchful eyes and a quiet air of tenacity. Auntie had a gentle face and a warm yet weary smile. I took a seat on the sofa, poking in my bag to arrange the gifts while the tea was served. The interior of the house had been modernized. It had plain white walls with simple stone counters, clean and functional, and an open common room.

Amanda had travelled alone on the first visit, with Lily as her guide. Uncle Mah seemed confused by the rest of us. He stared at Matt, looking him up and down. 'Very handsome,' Lily translated for Uncle Mah after they were introduced. Matt was over six feet tall and white. When the introductions came to Ying and me, Uncle Mah just nodded.

'Uncle Mah wants to know, have you received his letter?' Lily asked.

'Yes, I received it.' Amanda pulled it out of her bag and handed it to Lily. This was the first time I heard of the letter.

Lily carefully unfolded the pages of neatly written Chinese characters in black ink on white lined paper, dated December 2017, three months before. As Lily glanced through the contents, she suddenly looked very uncomfortable. 'Can anyone read this?'

'I think so, yes,' Amanda said.

'Oh,' Lily said uneasily. Uncle Mah hovered beside her and began to speak energetically, waving his hands in different directions.

'My friend tried to help me read it, but we didn't get too far,' Amanda said. 'What does it say?'

'So,' Lily began. 'After our visit last time, he wrote a summary of all that we found and what he remembered.' The first page, she said, was addressed to all the members of our family, and it outlined, in brief, Uncle Mah's memory of our family in the village:

There were indeed a Yue Gee, your grandfather, and Yue Gim in our village at the start of the twentieth century. They were the sons of Gee Su, your great-grandfather. The wife of Gee S, your great-grandmother, was known for her beauty. She had lived abroad before she fell ill, which brought her back to the village. She eventually died of an illness.

Your great-grandfather remarried Wong to take care of his children after his first wife died. The family lived in this village for a few years before migrating to Canada. After the Sino-Japanese War, your great-grandmother's second wife Wong bought some land. She killed herself during the Cultural Revolution for fear that she'd be publicly humiliated and tortured for owning some lands. Their houses were destroyed in 1968.

Amanda had told me about these revelations when we met at the hotel in Guangzhou. At first, I questioned the timeline. Uncle Mah would have been born around 1932, but our grandfather's family returned to Canada permanently before then. I was also puzzled about the story of our great-grandfather's second wife Wong. In his memoirs, our grandfather introduced Wong as an 'Aunt-Housekeeper', a widow who came to take care of the family in 1925 while his mother was dying. He wrote that his father had refused his mother's request to take Aunt Wong as a second wife or concubine

16

because it was 'highly improper for a Christian family to do so'.³

That night I skimmed back through the memoirs, which were saved on my laptop, and found confirmation of the second marriage. In 1935, our grandfather's last year of high school in Cranbrook, his father made a final solo trip to South Uplands, where he died of dysentery. Our grandfather learned about his father's death in a letter from clan relatives and 'found that widow Wong who came as a housekeeper had some sort of marriage agreement with Father before we left China so that she could have control of the house'.⁴ He never mentioned Aunt Wong's later death. She was, more or less, forgotten by our family, but she was the one who Uncle Mah remembered. Aunt Wong lived in our ancestral house for more than forty years before she died, two doors away from Uncle Mah.

I thought that this sad family story was what was bothering Lily. It disturbed me too, not so much the bare facts of death and illness, but the haunting silences that surrounded them. There was something else in the letter, though, that was amiss. As we sipped our tea, Uncle Mah urged Lily to continue reading.

Lily hesitated. 'So actually, he wrote this letter to you and everyone else who could be visiting. He wrote that it is great that we managed to find your ancestral home in Western Peaceful Place, but unfortunately, no one is living there anymore. The houses have been deserted for a long time. Some of them have even collapsed. It would be really kind of you if you could rebuild some houses in our village. He says he has few nieces and nephews who live in Canada. They are going to come back to the village to build some luxury new houses and have a big housewarming ceremony in January 2018. He suggests you contact them, and maybe you can even come with them on your next visit.' A few awkward moments followed. Here we were back in the village, just a few months after Uncle Mah sent the letter.

'So, you already missed it,' Lily said finally.

'Uncle Mah wants us to build houses?' I whispered to Amanda incredulously.

'Oh, yes, that's just because his son and his nephews built some houses here,' she said. 'They don't even use them.'

Uncle Mah started to talk enthusiastically about his nephews in Canada, emphasizing their contact details, which he had included in the letter. At the mention of Canadian relatives, Amanda perked up. She took out a photograph to show Uncle Mah, carefully pointing out her father, 'son of Yue Gee', and her siblings. Amanda was a few years younger than me, in her mid-thirties, and her hair was almost identical to mine, shoulder length and parted in the middle. Her father looked a lot like mine, but with a bigger smile.

On her first visit, Amanda brought a laminated photograph of our great-grandparents, grandfather, great-aunt and great-uncle taken in Cranbrook from 1928. Our great-grandmother's photograph, taken in 1924, was inset after her death to complete the family portrait. My family has a copy of the same photograph, and I always found it creepy, the idea of adding a dead person to a living portrait. Amanda showed this picture to everyone she met in the Mah villages in her quest to find someone who remembered Yue Gee.

'Do you have any photos of your family, Alice?' Amanda asked. 'To show Uncle Mah.'

'No, sorry,' I said. I did not think Uncle Mah would want to see pictures of my family.

'I know, I think I have some,' Amanda said, scrolling through her phone. After a few minutes she retrieved a family photo from my brother's wedding a few years before. She pointed out my father, another 'son of Yue Gee', and then my mother, white skinned with ash blonde hair. Uncle Mah's eyes widened, but he said nothing.

We stood up to gather our gifts. Matt brought out a video recorder to capture the special moment, so we could share it later with other Mah relatives. There are lots of heart-warming videos on the internet about people finding their ancestral villages in China. Many are from the third or fourth generation of overseas Chinese, like Amanda and me, searching for a connection with their roots.

Amanda presented Uncle Mah with the first gift, a carved black marble statue of a horse in an elegant green box. Mah (Ma) means 'horse' in Chinese. Mah statues and trinkets are common because the horse is one of the twelve signs of the Chinese zodiac. Uncle Mah smiled widely as he accepted the gift.

Next, Ying and I presented our small gifts and said that these were to share with the villagers. Or at least, I think we said that, or Lily must have said that. But maybe, looking back, we didn't.

Auntie laid the gifts out on a table, gently examining each in turn. I cringed at my clumsy selection as she turned the kitschy Scottie dog tins over in her hands.

'Doh je, doh je,' said Auntie and Uncle Mah, smiling and nodding at us.

'Thank you very much,' Lily translated ceremoniously.

It was a happy moment of gift-giving, but it already sowed the bad seeds of all that was to follow. Although we didn't know it yet, we were intruding on the most auspicious of occasions: Qingming, when people return to their home villages in China to sweep the tombs of their ancestors. We would not be building any houses, and we had no gifts left for the rest of the clan.

2. Eastern Clan Village

A car pulled up close behind us, honked and then swerved to pass along the narrow road. A few seconds later, another did the same. We followed Uncle Mah, who rode his motor scooter, wearing plain cotton clothes and a yellow helmet. We didn't know where he was leading us, not exactly. We knew it was to another Mah village some distance away, one of many in the region. After we finished our tea, Uncle Mah suddenly decided to take us there. He didn't offer a reason except that he hadn't been there in a long time.

The journey was excruciatingly slow. I wondered if Uncle Mah was aware of all the honks, and if he even remembered where he was going. But he seemed to have a clear sense of purpose. We drove past grassy hills covered in gravestones. I thought about the neglected tombs of my ancestors and tried to guess which hills they belonged to.

This time, I sat in the front seat next to Lily, and the others sat quietly in the back. Lily was younger than us, in her mid-twenties, with bobbed hair, black-rimmed glasses and a casual urban style. Recently, she had started her own business as a tourist guide, and one of her first customers was Amanda. Lily talked to fill the silence. As we turned down a long straight road towards the other Mah village, she spoke about the impact of the Cultural

Revolution on the older generation. Her grandma came from another Taishanese village in Guangdong.

'Even in the village, at a very young age they had very depressed times, so their behaviour, their way of dealing with things, is very aggressive,' Lily said.

The word 'aggressive' seemed oddly hard, and I felt the urge to soften it. 'But you don't feel that's the case with Uncle Mah,' I ventured.

'Hmmm,' Lily mumbled evasively and focused her attention on her driving, following Uncle Mah as he turned down another road.

I asked what she meant by aggressive. She thought for a moment and answered, 'It's like, my grandma, she always tells us to make money, marry a rich guy, it's very direct.'

During the Cultural Revolution, mass killings were widespread in rural villages across China, particularly in the South. More than half of the counties in Guangdong province reported collective killings between 1967 and 1968. According to the *Guangdong Province Gazetteer*, '42,237 died of unnatural causes due to random beatings, random killings, random detentions and random struggles.'[1] There were no Red Guards in the villages, like there were in the cities. Instead, as the sociologist Yang Su writes, 'neighbours killed neighbours'.[2] They pushed their 'class enemy' neighbours off cliffs and bludgeoned them with clubs and hoes.

We came to the entrance of the other Mah village. Two sturdy modern houses, one white and one red, stood on opposite sides of a small, paved square. Uncle Mah turned into the square and stopped. Another man on a scooter pulled up. He was middle aged and wore a black hooded sweatshirt and a baseball cap. Uncle Mah got off his scooter and lit a cigarette, greeting the man, who remained seated on the scooter. They began smoking and talking.

'The man is interested in what you are doing here, your intentions,' Lily told us. 'He asks if you still have relatives around this village or not.'

'No, I don't think so,' said Amanda.

'That's what Uncle Mah says, too,' said Lily, straining to listen. 'So, Uncle Mah says, "This village is a good place, and I know you have celebrities and smart people here." The other man says, "Yes, everywhere has people like that, of course we have them."'

They kept talking for a few minutes. We learned that this was known as the Eastern clan village, and it was rather big, with many small districts. Then we were ushered back into the car and instructed to follow the two men, who rode side-by-side into the village.

We were the celebrities and smart people of South Uplands, I realized, as I mulled over the snippets of translation. This was the reason for Uncle Mah's trip. We were the rich overseas returners, here in the flesh, for the other villagers to see. Everywhere has people like that, the man had said. That is, everywhere in the county of Taishan. More than a century since the first clan migrations to North America during the Gold Rush, Taishan was still known as the 'first home of overseas Chinese'. It relied heavily on 'silver letters' (or *qiaopi*), overseas money sent back to clan relatives from Gold Mountain, a tradition that hadn't quite come to an end.[3]

The road cut through rice fields before ascending into the hills. We stopped to look out over a lake surrounded by tall wispy trees. I posed for a photo, and everyone encouraged Uncle Mah to stand beside me, to get closer. The familiarity felt forced. In the photo, I am smiling awkwardly, and Uncle Mah is frowning.

We continued the tour, led by the two men on scooters, until we came to a concrete dam stretching over the lake. The men drove onto the top of the dam towards the dry hills on the other side. Hesitantly, Lily followed in the car. Within less than a minute, we came to a dead end. While we contemplated the precipice before us, the two scooters motored back to the middle of the dam, and a white van pulled up behind them. Uncle Mah and the other man on the scooter started talking, joined by half a dozen villagers from the van. The rest of us stayed in the car.

After a few minutes, there seemed to be some kind of disagreement between the villagers and Uncle Mah. Their voices became increasingly agitated, and I began to worry about the relations between the two villages. There was a long history of clan violence in Taishan, which included conflicts both between and within clans.

In the mid-nineteenth century, Taishan county was the main battlefield of the Hakka–Punti clan wars (1855–67), fought between the Punti ('people of the Earth') Han Chinese and the Hakka ('guest families') Chinese ethnic minority group, over access to land amid population expansion and drought. Roughly one million people died in the clan wars, and many more died due to famines and epidemics. The Hakka–Punti clan wars coincided with the Second Opium War, fought by Britain and France against the Qing dynasty to protect the lucrative opium trade in China, which was responsible for tens of millions of Chinese people becoming addicted to opium.[4] Alongside the poverty and violence, opium addiction in Taishan was rife. The Imperial Government finally suppressed the clan wars with brutal force, relocating most of the Hakka to different territories and leaving the ravaged lands of Taishan to the Punti. Over the ensuing decades, the main reason for such high levels of overseas migration from Taishan to North America was to escape from conflict and starvation. That, and the promise of gold.[5]

When the first Gold Mountain sojourners returned to Taishan to build lavish houses in the late nineteenth century, inspired by dreams of the West, they became targets for bandit attacks. Amid hunger and desolation, roving groups of destitute people wandered from village to village, plundering what they could. There were many kidnappings and occasional murders.[6]

'What's happening? Do they want something from us?' I asked Lily. She said no, they didn't, and not to worry about it. But I kept thinking about the houses that Uncle Mah wanted us to build and his boast that implied we were rich. I mentioned the houses, and she laughed nervously.

The discussions carried on at such length that it started to feel like we were being held there deliberately, perched on the edge of the dam, with no means of escape. Maybe I was misreading the situation, though, and the villagers were simply having a long friendly chat.

I remembered reading that the normal speaking volume of Taishanese is a shout, a harsh, rural dialect that was designed for survival, meant to carry over the fields.[7]

Eventually the villagers dispersed from the dam, and the other man on the scooter rode off. Lily inched the car forwards and backwards in a tight U-turn. If any dispute had taken place, Uncle Mah betrayed nothing. He rode back calmly over the dam and waited for us to follow. At first, we thought he might be leaving the village, but he had another goal in mind. He wove through the rolling landscape past leafy green fields in the afternoon sun until he came to a village square where a cluster of old brick houses faced a pond. Several men sat on the benches beside the pond, small children rode bicycles around the square, and a group of women stood next to the houses, drinking cold beverages. Uncle Mah stopped and beckoned for us to get out of the car.

The villagers observed us intently but pretended not to. Uncle Mah joined the men on the benches and watched a man shaping wood on an old machine lathe. After a few minutes, he wandered over to the group of women by the houses. We tagged along. There were six women in total, two older, two middle-aged and two younger women, one with a toddler resting over her shoulder. The mood was lively and buoyant. Uncle Mah began to speak with one of the older women, while Ying struck up a conversation with some of the others.

The woman who was speaking with Uncle Mah, Lily explained, was very happy. This year at Qingming, she would be allowed to sweep her ancestors' tombs for the first time. Previously, only men were allowed to observe this ritual, but now, women could do it too. This was different from other places in China, Lily said. As far as she could remember, women in her grandma's village were always allowed to sweep the tombs.

We lingered for a while, smiling politely, and waiting for cues about when it was time to leave. Amanda was frustrated at the length of this diversion and wanted to move on, but the visiting continued. Finally, Lily suggested that we go out for dinner at a local restaurant, one they had been to during their first visit with Uncle Mah.

We left the village in the fading evening light. I rode in the back seat, next to Ying, and she told me about her conversations with the villagers. 'They are all Mahs,' Ying confirmed. 'They say that they are all rich because they rely on overseas money. Some of the middle generation work in nearby paper, chemical and other factories. They are very proud of their village, and say it has the best water and best views and landscape.'

Just the day before, Ying and I had visited a petro-chemical village, located adjacent to industry on the urban periphery of Guangzhou, which bore a strange similarity to the Eastern clan village. It also had simple brick buildings overlooking a central pond. There too, we sensed the watchful gaze of the residents, who were proud of their village, noting that it was clean and inexpensive, with nice views of the pond. Except there, the village was in the shadow of a massive petrochemical complex, with its flaring smokestacks and catalytic crackers to refine chemicals from oil to make plastics. The air was heavy and acrid, unlike anything I had experienced before. I still carried it with me in my body: the pollution had obliterated my sense of smell.

It took nearly an hour to get to the restaurant. The place was cramped and smoky, and the dishes took a long time to arrive. There were palpable tensions in the air. Amanda was disappointed that our day had deviated from the plan. Ying was bothered by the smoke and by Amanda's fixation on the memoir, 'as if it was the Bible,' she told me. I was rattled too. I was disturbed by Uncle Mah's letter. Much as I tried, I could not get the fate of our great-grandfather's second wife Wong out of my mind. The matter-of-fact details in the letter somehow made it worse. I could not understand how Uncle Mah's appeal to build new houses followed from his confirmation of the suicide of our closest relative in the village.

I was also troubled by a question that was impossible to ask: did Uncle Mah, as Aunt Wong's neighbour, show any kindness to her during those terrible years of persecution?

At the end of the meal, Uncle Mah proposed that we host a dinner banquet for the villagers the next evening. During the first visit, Amanda had hosted a modest lunch banquet for one table of villagers. Uncle Mah proposed a larger banquet this time, for several tables of villagers. First, he suggested two tables, then three, and then settled at four. We shouldn't refuse, Lily advised us, because of cultural expectations, which had increased since the first visit, but she would try to keep the costs down.

On the drive to our hotel, we discussed the key piece of information that we had learned in the Eastern clan village: the annual Qingming festival was happening that very weekend, a week before elsewhere in China, not only there but in all the Mah villages of Taishan. Mahs from cities across China would return to their home villages to pay respect to their ancestors, sweeping their tombs and offering food, flowers and burnt paper money. Uncle Mah's son was about to arrive, and they would sweep the tombs the next day. We had not come prepared for this occasion.

'Maybe we could ask Uncle Mah if we could join him?' Amanda suggested hopefully. She had already told me about the failed attempt on their first visit to find our great-grandmother's tomb.

'I don't think that's a good idea,' Lily said. 'Qingming is for family members only. Besides, Uncle Mah was unhappy to hear that women are now allowed to sweep the tombs.'

For a moment, Amanda looked deflated, but then she brightened. While everyone was so busy with their tomb-sweeping, she decided, we could plan our own excursion in South Uplands the next day. It was our ancestral village too, and we would have it all to ourselves.

3. Hot Springs Hotel

The hot springs hotel sits at the top of a hill, a grand building tucked into the lush landscape. It is more of a resort than a hotel, with a warm wood interior, an hour's drive from the village. Most guests are Chinese tourists. We were a bit of an oddity, and Lily spent a long time at the reception desk negotiating the conditions of our stay.

'The PM 2.5 levels here are the same as in Guangzhou,' Ying reported with astonishment, scrolling through her phone. She had been tracking the daily particulate matter air pollution levels somewhat obsessively since her arrival in Guangzhou a month before. The PM 2.5 levels in Guangzhou were consistently high, but she had expected the countryside to have lower levels.

I was surprised too. My sense of smell was still gone, but I had the feeling that the air around me was simmering with substance, almost earthy in texture.

I felt an immediate sense of relief when I stepped into my room. The neatly laid bed and large picture window offered a minimalist aesthetic. In the hall wardrobe hung a white bathrobe and slippers, an alluring invitation. The hot springs were still open.

To reach the springs, you had to walk outside. By now it was dark. I followed the streams of people walking outside in their bathrobes, past the car park, along a path through grassy fields, towards an illuminated glass-covered building several hundred feet away.

I joined the queue in the building and scanned my hotel card at the front desk to access the baths. It was set up like a public swimming pool, with lockers and changing rooms, and a door leading outside to the baths.

As I entered the cool night air, I was struck by the stars, just visible in the hazy purple sky. I breathed in deeply, marvelling at the tiny points of ancient light. Seeing the stars reminded me of my family far away, looking up at the same sky from different places and times. The next thing that hit me was smoke, wafting across my path in little plumes. Some of the guests were smoking as they manoeuvred around the baths.

The only hot springs I had visited before were in British Columbia, on a family holiday as a child. They had seemed magical, with natural pools of thermal water nestled in the boreal spruce forest. By contrast, this hotel's hot springs felt artificial and constrained, with tiled baths, stone paths and carefully landscaped features. There was an array of baths, each with different temperature ranges and minerals, as well as a water park for children, and some massage and relaxation treatments. I craved a bath with intense heat, the kind where you need to immerse your body inch by inch just to tolerate the pain of submersion. But I also wanted to find a quiet place. I wandered around until I found a bath that was unoccupied.

Slowly, I slipped into the warm water and gazed up at the starlit sky, framed by the silhouettes of trees. I have no religion, but there is a ritual that I like to perform when I travel to a new place, which helps me to feel more connected. It comes from an idea I once read in a children's book, that the spirit cannot travel any faster than at a walking pace, so it takes a while for the spirit to catch up with the body. My ritual is simply to imagine how far away my spirit is from my body at a given time. At this moment, I imagined that my spirit was probably somewhere just off the east coast of England. It would never catch up, given the length of my stay in China.

Across different cultures, hot springs are believed to have healing powers. Yet I recalled from my research that hot spring hotels, which are popular tourist attractions throughout China, are also associated with elevated levels of radon, an odourless, invisible radioactive gas that is released from rocks, minerals and soils. Hot spring waters have naturally high concentrations of radon, which can pose health risks to hotel workers and tourists, including lung damage and cancer.[1]

The potential radioactive threat reminded me of the Taishan Nuclear Plant under construction nearby. Bizarrely, hot spring resorts are often located in direct proximity to toxic industry in China. In 2003, a major petrochemical industry park in Jiangsu discovered geothermal resources adjacent to the park, and they worked together with local authorities to create hot spring resorts in the area, rebranding the city as a hot spring destination.[2]

Years of studying toxic landscapes had put me on high alert, and I found it difficult to relax.

I doubt that my ancestors would have visited these

hot springs. Even if the springs existed in some form nearly a century ago, they were too far away. Travel between villages was done on foot. Shortly after their arrival in the Mah village, my grandfather's family embarked in sedan chairs to visit his dying mother's own clan village, carried by local men. It took them half a day to reach the village. My grandfather remembered his mother embracing her relatives and crying over her illness. A few days later, his mother passed away.

I was alone with my thoughts for no more than a few minutes before a young man and woman with two small children entered the bath. I tried to get by with just a short greeting, but the woman spoke English and wanted to know where I came from and what I was doing there.

'I am visiting my ancestral village,' I said. 'I come from Canada, and my father's family comes from a Mah clan village in Taishan.'

'Ah,' the woman said, smiling. 'My husband is also a Mah. He comes from Green Vines. We are also here for Qingming.'

Green Vines was the market town closest to our family village. We planned to visit it the next day. I was grateful for this small connection.

When I returned to my hotel room, I could not sleep. I kept thinking about the coincidence of our trip with Qingming. Of course, it was me and not fate who had chosen the dates of our trip, timed around a tight research schedule. Still, it seemed like a sign. I was not sure whether it was an auspicious one or not.

4. Tomb-Sweeping Day

By dawn there were itchy red bumps all over my arms and ankles. Dozens of mosquitoes clung to the walls. It was Qingming, also known as Tomb-Sweeping Day, just like my dad said was the custom. In truth, I had no desire to sweep any tombs. Our family's house was destroyed, and our ancestors' tombs were lost. Anyway, if we were going to go with tradition, it was sons who had the duty to maintain the lineage. Daughters would be married off to other clans.

We left for South Uplands after breakfast, an ample buffet of rice porridge, egg pancakes and steamed buns. Ying stayed behind in the hot springs; she had seen enough of the village already. PM 2.5 levels were still high, she said, bordering on unhealthy. The morning sky was thick with clouds, and the hills of Taishan looked bleak and subdued. I lost count of the small villages we passed that resembled our own. Many had bandit towers, reminiscent of castle turrets in medieval Europe, for warning off intruders.

At the gateway arch, we stopped to take some selfies. Matt said Amanda and I looked like sisters, with our long dark hair and similar features. The gateway arch was pale green and glossy pink, with ornate little drag-ons on top, out of sync with the weary look of the village.

Beyond it, a ploughing machine stood in the middle of the narrow road between the rice fields.

When we entered the main village square, we were greeted by a man in loose grey cotton clothes who was packing up a car with an entire barbecued pig. The man recognized Amanda and Lily. He was the one who had helped them to find our subdivision, Western Peaceful Place.

'This man is going with his family for their Qingming ceremony,' Lily said. 'He asks if you would like to join them.'

'Thank you, but we have other plans,' Amanda said, sounding pleased to be asked. But the man did not offer again, and I do not think that his invitation was serious. People are not supposed to participate in other families' tomb-sweeping because it brings bad luck.

Our plan was to go for a walk in the village. Qing-ming means 'clean and bright' in Chinese, marking the beginning of spring and the farming season. During Qingming, people honour nature as well as ancestors, spending time walking outside and enjoying the spring blossoms.

We walked a short distance east, where our great-great-grandfather was said to have had a house, from where the village may have been originally built, where the now-defunct railway line came in. Next, west in the direction of our subdivision, we came to the village clan hall.

Mottled white and grey with ageing stonework, the clan hall was built in the extravagant Western style typical of early twentieth-century Taishan. It had balconies lined with Romanesque arches, four main pillars, and a façade carved with floral and Chinese characters, including the traditional character for Mah (馬). There was a large open central doorway leading into a dark interior, and bales of rice straw were stacked outside beneath the balconies. On the top was the Five-star Red Flag of the People's Republic of China.

'This is the clan hall that was made from the bricks of our house,' Amanda told me.

It was the third time I had heard the clan hall story. Uncle Mah recounted the original story during the first visit, but I heard only the repeated versions, stripped of any detail.

'You know, in the Cultural Revolution, clan halls like this one were sites of torture,' Lily said in a low voice. 'People would be brought here for struggle sessions and public humiliation.'

This was new information. We stood before the clan hall rather solemnly for a few moments. I found it chilling, to say the least, especially the gaping door. I imagined the cloud of terror hovering over our ancestral house after Aunt Wong's death; the house being dismembered, brick by brick, like a horse carcass picked apart by black vultures; and the grey bricks meticulously reassembled into the body of the hall. Given its size, the clan hall could not have been built from the bricks of our house alone. Perhaps it was a composite of multiple houses expropriated from other 'disloyal' overseas families.

We carried on past the central village along the road

to Western Peaceful Place through thickets of banana trees and rows of freshly planted vegetables. The overcast sky was glaringly bright, and we walked briskly, swatting at the mosquitoes. Among the weeds at the side of the road there was a tiled pedestal with a miniature pagoda roof, which proclaimed that the area was a farmland protection zone. This meant that the village land was protected by the state for agricultural use, for reasons of food security, Lily said, and it could not be developed for other uses.

'Here we are, back to the junction,' Amanda said as we approached the red and white house at the entrance to Western Peaceful Place. 'Everyone will probably be gone for Qingming.' But to our surprise, it was much busier than the day before, with several cars parked near the main gathering place and families with small children wandering around in the long grass.

An elderly woman came out of the house and invited us to sit outside for tea. Her name was Auntie Fan, and she and her husband had met Amanda and Lily before. Auntie Fan was about seventy years old, with short thinning hair and a stern expression. She had been the one to introduce them to Uncle Mah, since he was the oldest person in the subdivision and had the greatest chance of remembering our family's history.

Auntie Fan served us tea in thin disposable plastic cups, the kind that are designed only for cold beverages, 'never hot,' a petrochemical industry executive once told me. The next time we came, Auntie Fan said, we should make sure to contact her too. Uncle Mah had not told Auntie Fan about our visit, like Lily thought he would. Her grandma's village was more communal, and they always shared news and gifts. While we sipped our tea, several cars pulled into the junction, mostly young families arriving for Qingming. A few stopped to say hello.

The next thing I knew, the Polaroid camera came out, and I felt the urge to hide. For some reason, Amanda and Matt believed that the villagers were fascinated by Polaroid cameras and that photos made ideal gifts. This was, at least in my view, an embarrassing assumption. A few of the villagers gathered around as Matt demonstrated the Polaroid printer. He had a light-hearted, affable manner, and the villagers seemed to enjoy the performance.

I was relieved when Amanda suggested that we walk to the site where our family's house used to be, while Matt and Lily stayed behind to print the photos.

Beyond the junction, it was quiet. I enjoyed the chance to take things in slowly – the pond, a lone tree, and bundles of twigs and branches I hadn't noticed before. After a few minutes, we came to the lane past Uncle Mah's house and through to the far side of it, which overlooked the rice fields. His house was the first in the original row of houses of Western Peaceful Place. Two doors down, to the west, was the site of our former ancestral home.

A simple two-storey house stood where ours had once been. It was built half a century later than the houses on either side, but it looked more decrepit. The house had the same patchy appearance of the clan hall, weathered white and dark grey. The only decorative feature was a crudely latticed concrete balcony, which was blackened and sagged in the middle. All six of the windows had broken panes, and a retractable security grille covered the front door.

The house gave me the same hollow feeling as the clan hall, like I was looking at despair itself.

'Isn't it amazing, how it doesn't seem to have changed at all since Grandpa's time?' Amanda exclaimed.

Startled, I turned around, and took a moment to adjust to Amanda's view. She was looking out across the rice fields. The watery squares of rice shoots reflected the pearl grey sky, and the distant hills hummed in muted tones of blue and green.

I nodded and smiled. 'Except for the power lines,' I said.

That morning at breakfast, Amanda asked me what I wanted to see most in the village. This was it. To stand in this place, where our grandfather and his family once stood, looking out at the fields and the hills, knowing that this is where our family comes from, and the place is still here, and we have found it, and we can be here, despite all that has been lost, just for a moment.

The moment did not last long. Lily and Matt came up behind us, together with Uncle Mah.

'Uncle Mah and his wife want to invite us to lunch,' Lily told us.

'Oh, but we were planning to go to a restaurant in Green Vines,' said Amanda.

'They say Green Vines is too busy with the festival, and the food will take too long,' Lily countered.

We refused three times before accepting, which Lily assured us was the custom.

On the table for lunch were some leftovers from the meal the night before, as well as some chicken feet and thighs. I am a vegetarian, but I ate as much as I could stomach, picking around the bones and the cartilage and skin. We could hear the chickens squawking outside as we ate.

'Auntie says that Chinese people believe the thigh is the best part,' Lily said. 'It is always reserved for the youngest member of the family.'

'That would be me,' Amanda grinned and tucked into the thigh.

After lunch, it was time for tea. Uncle Mah brought out one of the British telephone box tins.

'Uncle Mah wants to know, there is lots of good tea in China, so what is special about the tea you brought?' Lily asked me.

'Oh,' I said, taken aback. There was nothing special about the tea I had brought, and in fact, it was probably low quality. 'Well, it is black tea,' I ventured, 'which is something that English people like to drink in the afternoon.'

Auntie served us the telephone box tea, and we all sampled it dutifully. Lily wrinkled her nose. 'This is not as good as Chinese tea,' she said.

While we finished our tea, Uncle Mah began to speak rather insistently with Lily. Something was on his mind.

'Uncle Mah feels guilty because he has not helped you enough, and you are so kind and brought so many nice presents,' Lily told us. 'He is very sad that you no longer have a house in the village.' Then she repeated Uncle Mah's request for us to build a new house. Somehow, I knew this would come up again.

'Thanks,' Amanda responded. 'Tell Uncle Mah that is very nice, but there is no need to feel sad about it, it's okay.'

But it was not okay, and Lily looked worried. 'Uncle Mah says it is so kind of you to bring presents for him, but you should also buy some fruits to share with the villagers,' she said. 'We can go to Green Vines.'

We thanked Uncle Mah and Auntie for lunch and set out for the local market town to buy some fruits for the clan. How could we have been so thoughtless to show up on Qingming, of all days, empty-handed?

5. Oranges and Goose

When we reached Green Vines, we parked in a dusty lot strewn with rubble, next to a farmer's field and a modern bank. Across the road was a fruit and vegetable stand, where we bought some oranges, a symbol of good luck and prosperity, to take back to the clan.

The town had the distinctive Taishanese air of decaying splendour. Trees stretched from the cracked roofs of concrete buildings, and a jumble of awnings covered the streets. The market was festive, packed with vendors selling Qingming specialities: rice pastries, pretend money, incense and firecrackers. Lily suggested we try the sticky rice buns, which were sweet and eggy.

In my grandfather's childhood, Bak Sha was a place of enchantment. Market days were held every ten days, attracting hawkers and entertainers from across the region. There were dancing monkeys, snake charmers and acrobats. Live fish and shrimp were brought in from the coast over the hills and sold in tanks of salt water.

Yet despite its allure, Bak Sha left only vague impressions in my mind. I was too distracted. Why was Uncle Mah so insistent that we build a house in the village? Why did he say he felt guilty?

Lily was perplexed about this too, and she tried to offer an explanation. 'In traditional Chinese culture,' she said, 'houses are the resting place for the spirit, so it would be distressing not to have an ancestral house.' As we strolled into the town, she told a story about a man from her grandma's village who lived in Hawaii and had not lived in his home village for forty years. Recently, he sent money to build a new house in the village in Taishan. He never even set foot in it. The villagers said it was because he needed a house for his spirit.

I could almost picture what it would be like, if we had that kind of money, building a new house in the village in honour of our ancestors, tearing down the ruins and starting fresh, even having a housewarming party, like Uncle Mah wrote in his letter, inviting all the aunts, uncles and cousins, restoring our place in the village. Except that we were migrant families, the descendants of restless spirits, gone for too long without a resting place. There was a darkness inside me, a resistance to happy stories. If houses were infused with spirits, then what happened to Aunt Wong's?

At a market stall, Amanda chose some tropical fruits for the clan, some of her local favourites. A young woman with long hair riding a motor scooter stopped by to greet us. She was Auntie Fan's daughter, out doing some shopping, and she recognized Amanda from her previous visit. She said she was looking forward to the banquet we would be hosting that evening. I had almost forgotten about the banquet. As the daughter rode off, Lily tutted at Amanda's choice of fruit. It was fine to eat at home but not so lucky to share on Qingming.

On our way back to Western Peaceful Place, Amanda

wanted to stop by another Mah village just across the road, where some of our grandfather's relatives once lived. Amanda had been to the village before, early in her search to find our own. It was located on a hillside, with neat rows of houses extending up the slope. I thought we were coming just to look around, but Amanda wanted to do some visiting.

'Last time we were here, we met a ninety-year-old man who said he remembered meeting Grandpa,' she said. 'Let's see if we can find him. I think I remember the way.'

'But if the man is ninety years old, then he could not have met our grandfather,' I objected.

Amanda wanted to visit the man anyway. She had fond recollections of her last visit and thought of this man, like Uncle Mah, as a relation. We followed her as she strode up and down the stone lanes between the houses, trying to locate the man's house. After a few minutes, one of the neighbours came out and said that the man we were looking for was very frail and could no longer walk, and he was resting in bed.

'Okay then, we should leave,' I said, turning back down the lane. But the neighbour had a key for the man's house, and he invited us inside, offering to help the man out of bed.

We waited in the front room of the house. I found it difficult to sit still, not knowing what to do, mortified at the invasion of privacy. The man was clearly unwell, and we could hear him grunt in the room beside us as he struggled to get out of bed. Amanda seemed entirely at ease, as if we were visiting an ailing family member who would appreciate our company. She reflected on how the layout of this house was very similar to what our great-grandfather's would have looked like, given the age of the house and the style, based on our grandfather's descriptions in the memoirs. The house had a dividing wall with an archway in the middle, and symmetrical sides, with an altar on the top part of the front room loft, and bedrooms and a stove in the back.

About fifteen minutes later, the man, his legs thin and trembling, stepped into the room, supported by the neighbour, looking at us with a dazed expression. He sat down on a chair and said nothing at first, coughing and straining to focus. Then, slowly, the man said that he remembered Amanda, and she smiled and mentioned the 'Mah brothers', Yue Gee and Yue Gim. At this, the man paused and said that he did not think he remembered meeting our grandfather and his brother after all. It was another pair of brothers he was thinking of, soldiers, from the time of the Sino-Japanese War.

The front door opened, and a man of about sixty entered the room carrying heavy plastic bags. The elderly man's son and family were home from their tomb-sweeping outing, bringing barbecued goose and other leftover foods. We got up to leave, but they insisted we stay and laid out some goose on a paper plate. The goose strips were still warm, cut about the length of a hand, and covered in layers of white fat. Lily brought out some of the oranges to share.

By now it was half past three, long after Uncle Mah

was expecting us to return, and I started to feel anxious because, at this rate, we would spend the entire rest of Qingming in this family's home and run out of time to share the fruits with the other Mah villagers. Amanda said I should relax, that I was becoming too British.

The elderly man still had a copy of a Polaroid photo of himself and Amanda from the first visit, which was displayed on the wall behind us. I guess there was a meaningful connection after all, and it proved to be a good exit strategy. Matt took another photo of everyone and printed it out as a parting gift.

On the drive back to Green Vines, we watched the families gathered along the hillside graves burning paper money and laying willow branches and fruits.

'What do people believe will happen if they don't sweep their ancestors' tombs every year?' I asked Lily.

'Oh,' she said with a slight frown. 'N-nothing.'

6. The Gifts

By the time we returned to Western Peaceful Place, there were few villagers in sight, just Auntie Fan and a small group of younger people sitting in front of a nearby house. Uncle Mah had come and waited for us but then left again. Lily called to tell him we were back. Meanwhile, Amanda presented Auntie Fan with two plastic bags full of fruit. Auntie Fan peered into the bags with a dismissive look and gestured for us to sit down on the low concrete benches under one of the trees.

It was only then that I noticed how extensive the exposed roots of the tree were, stretching towards the sky as if pulled by an invisible force. It was a banyan tree, a symbol of immortality due to its strange aerial roots, and a prominent feature of many rice villages in Taishan. Situated next to the path leading into the village, the banyan tree is an important gathering place for villagers to share gossip and news.[1]

Auntie Fan sat next to Lily and began to speak in a distinctly unfriendly manner. After a few minutes, Uncle Mah arrived up the path from his house, but he did not approach us and chose to sit on a bench under another tree, behind us, smoking a cigarette.

'Aiyahh!' Lily suddenly leaned forward and cupped her head in her hands. We asked if she was okay. She pressed her palms into her eyes and her fingertips into her scalp, and then lifted herself up with a laugh and a slight grimace. 'So, uh, Auntie Fan thanks you for the fruits,' she said at last. 'She says the fruits are very nice, but they are not as nice as the presents you brought for Uncle Mah.' Lily's first language was Cantonese, and she had learned Taishanese from her grandma, but she struggled with some of the expressions. It was difficult for her to translate what Auntie Fan wanted to tell us, she said, because of cultural differences.

After much hesitation, Lily managed to come up with a translation, although it was clear that she left some parts out. The problem bothering Auntie Fan, she explained, was this: there was an elderly woman in the village who walked with a cane, who had not been able to come to the lunch during Amanda's last visit. Unfortunately, because of her health, the woman would not be able to come to the dinner that evening and was very upset about missing out a second time. All the other villagers were also unhappy because they did not think it was fair that we gave all our presents to Uncle Mah and nothing to them. Uncle Mah was not related to us any more directly than they were. Auntie Fan did not accept Lily's explanation that the presents we had brought were for all the villagers to share. She insisted that, at the very least, we should give the elderly woman with the cane a red pocket to compensate for missing the lunch and the dinner.

Both Amanda and I were familiar with red pockets, but only in a Chinese Canadian context. Growing up,

48

our grandparents used to give us red pockets of 'lucky money' as presents. A red pocket (*hongbao*) is a small red envelope filled with money and decorated with Chinese symbols or characters for luck and prosperity. Traditionally, grandparents, parents and other married adults give red pockets to children and unmarried younger relatives on special occasions. I always thought it was done just for novelty, as a nicer way of presenting a gift of money than taping it inside a Hallmark card. It had never occurred to me to give one to someone myself.

As if on cue, an elderly woman with a cane walked up the path into the meeting place. She was just over four feet tall, with short grey hair and gently stooped shoulders, and she had a lost look about her. She took a seat on the bench beside Auntie Fan, her body almost weightless in comparison. Astonished, Lily whispered that this was the very woman Auntie Fan was talking about, as if we had not already guessed.

Amanda interpreted this whisper as an instruction. She reached into her handbag and brought out her wallet, revealing a thin wad of crisp banknotes. She pulled out a 100 Chinese renminbi note (the equivalent of about 11 British pounds) and a red pocket, which she happened to be carrying with her, before Lily realized what she was doing.

'Hide it, hide it!' Lily hissed.

Quickly, Amanda turned away from the woman, in the direction of Uncle Mah, who was watching us silently. She stuffed the note inside the red pocket and slipped her wallet back into her handbag.

Turning back to face the woman, with a small bow and both hands outstretched, Amanda presented her with the red pocket.

From where I was sitting, facing Amanda, I was not able to see the expression on the woman's face. Lily said afterwards that she looked like a child receiving candy, very happy. Almost immediately, though, the woman's expression changed, and she asked, 'But why should only I get a red pocket? You should give everyone a red pocket.' Auntie Fan nodded in agreement, that this was the fair thing to do. Red pocket in hand, the woman with the cane stood up to leave, slowly making her way back down the path.

Lily's face, normally open and smiling, grew contorted, her eyes darting around. I felt like I was seeing her for the first time. How had I not noticed the strain that she was under? Translation is exhausting work. Suspended between worlds, pulled in different directions, trying to hold a centre. Everyone in the village would soon know about the red pocket, Lily said in a desperate voice, and they would want to have one too.

Under the taut, wiry branches of the banyan tree, we had a long conversation in English about the red pockets. Auntie Fan sat quietly, listening, her face sullen. She did not understand our words, but she knew exactly what we were talking about.

We should not have given the red pocket to the woman, Lily lamented, even though Auntie Fan had asked us to. For the sake of fairness, we would now be expected to give each person at the dinner that evening a red pocket with 100 renminbi, in addition to hosting the dinner. We did not know how many villagers to expect. Thirty, perhaps forty. The dinner was in less than two hours. But where could we get that many red pockets in time? Whatever we did, Lily warned, we had to be discreet. If word got around that we would be giving out red pockets, who knew how many would come.

In fact, both Uncle Mah and Auntie Fan had been asking Lily to tell us to give red pockets to all the villagers since our arrival, but Lily had not wanted to. In China, she said, money carries a different meaning in comparison with other kinds of gifts, and as soon as we gave money, the expectation would be much higher the next time. If we gave the villagers 100 renminbi this time, then next time we returned, we would need to give 200 renminbi. But Uncle Mah and Auntie Fan kept insisting, repeating the request several times. Throughout the day, Lily kept telling Uncle Mah and Auntie Fan that it was not in our culture to give red pockets. After we revealed our knowledge about red pockets, though, the situation changed.

Lily had never heard of giving red pockets to anyone other than very close relatives. She thought it sounded greedy and strange. I think she felt protective of Amanda, seeing her as innocent, like a small bird alone in a nest. A few days later, over coffee in Shenzhen, Lily told me that her boyfriend, who had been the driver on their first trip to the village, had explicitly warned her never to give the villagers any money. He had some knowledge of Taishanese culture and did not trust Uncle Mah.

In overseas ancestral villages in China, I learned later, gifts of red pockets are not uncommon. Lily's grandma was from a village in Taishan, but not one like ours, where most villagers have overseas ancestors or relatives. Since the reopening of China to foreign tourists in the 1980s, many overseas Chinese, known as *huaqiao* or 'Chinese sojourners', have returned to their home villages during festivals to visit relatives and elders, bringing gifts and red pockets filled with 50 or 100 renminbi (also known as *yuan*, worth anywhere between 5 and 12 British pounds depending on currency fluctuations).[2] The most affluent and devoted among the sojourners build new houses and restore the old, leaving them unused after they depart. Gradually, the houses fall into states of disrepair, repeating the cycle.[3]

Between the nineteenth and twentieth centuries, *qiaopi* remittance letters from overseas Chinese relatives were crucial for the survival of many families in China, especially in Taishan, the 'home of overseas Chinese'. Today, *qiaopi* are inscribed in the UNESCO Memory of the World Register, as part of the world's documentary heritage.[4] Over 170,000 *qiaopi* sent from overseas Chinese in North America, Southeast Asia and Oceania have been collected in archives and museums throughout China.[5]

'What should we do? I think we should bring the red pockets,' I said.

'Yes, I know all about the expectations about gifts in China,' Amanda replied, with a curious touch of nostalgia. 'My mom used to warn us about this when we visited the relatives.'

I felt a sudden pang of longing at Amanda's ease with the village and its traditions. The fact that the villagers wanted more gifts from us was something she could relate to, a source of comfort. Personally, I could not relate to these cultural traditions; I only sensed the unhappiness beneath. My dad seldom spoke about his Chinese roots, apart from stories centred around food: memories of fighting with siblings over who got to eat the lucky fisheye; family gatherings at dim sum restaurants; and a lifelong love of duck.

Amanda grew up in a family with two Chinese Canadian parents, and she had been searching to reconnect with her Chinese heritage for several years, since her mother passed away. It was frustrating to grow up looking but not speaking Chinese, she said, especially alongside more recent migrants from China. I think my dad must have felt similar when he was a youth in suburban Toronto. He often seemed uncomfortable on our visits to Chinatown when people spoke to him in Chinese. Finding the Mah village really did feel like coming home for Amanda, the culmination of months of travel in China, trying to understand the language and culture.

I could see that Amanda's yearning for connection came partly from grief, and that it followed her. But maybe some unknown pain was following me too.

7. The House

I did not want to go inside. I felt a recoiling, a revul-
sion, at the thought of crossing into the house. It
exuded something cold and morbid that I did not want
to touch.

While we were chatting under the tree, Uncle Mah
had gone away and come back again. He announced that
the woman to whom we had given the red pocket wanted
to invite us into her house, the one on the site of our
former ancestral home, which she owned but did not
live in. The woman's papery, freckled hands trembled as
she brought out the key. The sliding metal grille in front
of the door was so rustys it could scarcely move along
its rails. A few of the villagers hovered outside to watch
the spectacle. I held back as the others went in, first
Amanda, then Matt, then Lily. Through the half-open
doorway, I could see the small-framed woman glance up
at something on the right-hand wall, above her, with
her mouth slightly open. Her eyes had a faraway look,
somewhere between sorrow and devotion.

Do I have to enter? A tingling sensation across my
upper arms told me not to. It would be like stepping into
the filmset of a single confined space, reeling across
centuries of human drama. I did not want to see those
pictures, nor play a part. The roof could come crashing

down. But I could not refuse, as I understood that the invitation was offered in the spirit of a gift.

As I crossed the threshold, I followed the woman's gaze towards a photograph of a young man hanging on the wall, framed in black. The man had a long thin face, a faint smile and neatly combed black hair. The image was so faded that his face appeared indistinct, difficult to focus on. Under the photograph were two pale orange sheets of paper covered in Chinese handwriting, taped to the wall, and a simple wooden table beneath, with little red pots of incense and glass bottles arranged in a semi-circle.

'Is this her husband?' Matt asked Lily, pointing at the photo. One of the villagers responded that it was her son, but we should not talk about it.

'Oh, okay,' Matt said. Lily laughed, because immediately after telling us not to talk about it, the villager told everyone that we had asked about the photo of the son.

The inside of the house seemed frozen, with all the living objects stuck in place, as though it had been abandoned in haste after a nuclear disaster. I retreated as soon as I could, outside towards the moving air, nodding my thanks to the woman, who remained transfixed by her son.

Through the narrow opening past the grille, we came out onto the strip of concrete pavement between the old brick houses and the rice fields, among scattered stones and piles of kindling. It reminded me of derelict docklands, but on an intimate scale. Uncle Mah was engrossed in a discussion with Auntie and three of the villagers, gesturing at different houses along the row.

Recalling our earlier moment together in this place, I asked Amanda what she liked most about her first visit.

'It was when Uncle Mah remembered the story of our family,' she said. 'And I knew that I had finally found our village.' At first, when she showed Uncle Mah the photos of our grandfather and his family, he did not say anything. Instead, he gave her a tour of Western Peaceful Place, pointing out the different buildings and trying to guess which one could have been our great-grandfather's. But then, on passing the site of our former family house, a light seemed to switch on, and he started to recall the story of our great-grandmother who was very beautiful and who had died of illness, and the two sons and the second wife Wong. He described our family story without any prompting, and it echoed the details from the memoirs. There was no doubt that it was a genuine memory, which Lily confirmed.

Now, Uncle Mah wanted to give us another tour of Western Peaceful Place, to show us the best spot to build a new house. He had some proposals. Proposal One: we could purchase the house back from the woman whose house we had just visited, demolish it and rebuild on the site of our great-grandfather's house. Pointing at roof-tops bursting with weeds, Uncle Mah told us that the houses on either side of our ancestral house once belonged to our great-grandfather's two brothers.

Amanda tried to change the topic. She urged me to ask Uncle Mah some questions about our family. She wanted me to have the opportunity to do so, just like she had.

I struggled to think of something that would be appropriate to ask. 'Maybe,' I said to Lily, 'you could ask Uncle Mah what he remembers about growing up as a child or a young man in this village, and if he could describe what he liked best about growing up here?'

Lily translated my question for Uncle Mah. A lengthy discussion followed, with lots of back and forth and laughter between Uncle Mah, Auntie and the three villagers, two middle-aged women and an older man, each dressed in light shirts and black trousers. At least this was convivial, not hostile, and it came as a relief.

'We've got to get the English translation,' Matt finally said.

'Okay,' Lily said. 'So, I was trying to ask him, but Uncle Mah keeps telling you about where the best place is to build a house.' She laughed apologetically. 'But I got the information from Uncle Mah's wife about why she married Uncle Mah, which is because her father said that this is a nice village. Before they got married, they didn't know each other, so she is from another village. Before she married, she heard from her father that this village, even though it is small, is very open.'

While Lily was speaking, Uncle Mah continued talking with the other villagers. He waved west, beyond our ancestral house, towards a stand of leafy semi-tropical trees.

'He is still thinking about where the best place is to build. He will just continue. Now, this is the best place! He will show you the best place, for now.'

'Real estate, real estate,' Amanda sighed.

'In sociology, that's also often what happens with interviews,' I said, trying to lessen her disappointment. 'You want to find out something, but you learn about something else, but it still tells you something.'

'Yeah, sure,' she said.

'It tells you what has meaning for people.'

Proposal Two: we could build a house at the end of the row of five houses overlooking the pond, towards the very start of Western Peaceful Place. Uncle Mah walked off towards this second site, which was located on a patch of weeds and rocks.

'This is the head of the land,' Lily said. 'The first place is always the nicest place. Now, this is a nice place to build a house. In the Chinese mind, the best place to build a house is with the mountains to the back and facing the water. I have the back out, always, and I have money inside, in front of me. Water stands for money, so you see, all the villages have the small ponds in the centre.'

Amanda gave Lily an exasperated look. A sturdy, round-faced woman wearing blue gumboots walked past us, leading a water buffalo with a long green rope.

'Just a second, I will try to guide him,' Lily said.

'To talk about the opposite of house building,' Amanda said emphatically.

I tried to think of another question to ask, to please Amanda. But I could not think of one, and Uncle Mah wandered off again, further still, towards the far end of the subdivision. He brought us to an old brick building with the characters for 'Western Peaceful Place' carved in speckled concrete above a wooden door, next to the water's edge. It had a faded stone star at the top. There were no signs of present use, and it looked peaceful, true to its name.

Proposal Three: we could build a house on a new plot of land. Uncle Mah pointed back towards the disconsolate row of houses, gesturing towards the possibilities for renewal. In this moment, I felt the weight of obligation, as if we could mend the ruptures of the past, clear out the damaged remnants. But to whom were we obliged?

'I think you should write a story about these people here,' Lily told me.

Only later, on the flight from Guangzhou back to London, did I realize that there were some questions that I could have asked Uncle Mah. One question was about our great-grandfather's death in the village, and the whereabouts of his tomb, which Amanda must have missed, because she only asked after our great-grandmother's tomb. This second death was buried in the memoirs, amid descriptions of school. Our grandfather wrote that, in his final year of high school, he suffered from poor marks in two of his examinations because he wrote them under strain just after hearing of his father's death in China. The news came from a letter by his uncle, which took about a month to arrive, in 1935. His father's death was sparsely described, in comparison with that of his mother, but it was more recent, ten years later. Uncle Mah was too young to remember either death, but it was interesting that his 'genuine' recollection, summoned from collective memory, was only of the first.

Another question was about the fate of our closest relative in the village. When our grandfather was writing his memoirs in the late 1980s, he learned that the village elders 'decided our family house was unduly taken as we were not disloyal and offered compensation which was assigned to our closest relative there, the widow of a cousin, brother of Jack'.[1] Who was the widow of the cousin? Someone must remember her too. From the conversations that followed, I doubt it would have made any difference. As Lily put it bluntly, we were not seen as kin, but as banks.

8. The Banquet

From the beginning, I was searching for a connection. On the flight to Guangzhou, in the streets of the old city, in the hot springs, in the village. Here, in an ordinary Chinese restaurant in Bak Sha, I found one. To be sitting around a large revolving table, alongside ten people with satisfied smiles and chopsticks poised, felt deeply familiar, almost comfortable. Somehow, the people around the table looked more like the Chinese Canadians I grew up with than in any other place, almost like they were family.

The red pockets seemed to bring us together, Amanda and I, something definitive that could be grasped. Before dinner, Lily drove to Green Vines to buy some red pockets. Next, she shuttled groups of elderly villagers to the restaurant, which was a ten-minute drive away, and she collected Amanda, Matt and me last. When Lily collected us, she slipped us the red pockets, and we sat in the back seat together, stuffing the pockets as fast as we could through the turns and bumps. Amanda was more skilful at folding the notes, from years of practice doing fundraising campaigns as a girl guide. We didn't manage to finish in time, and when we parked outside the restaurant, Lily warned us to keep the pockets out of sight. We crouched in our seats beneath the car window. It felt strangely conspiratorial, huddled in the back seat together, filling red pockets with cash.

The restaurant looked like the one we had been to the evening before, except bigger. Most of the guests had already arrived. We sat at the third table, the furthest from the door, with Uncle Mah, who was resting his arm on the back of his chair, watching the action at the other two tables, and smoking. Lily was worried because the food had been ordered by the villagers already, and they had gone for the highest-level banquet possible, which included numerous sumptuous dishes, as well as brandy, coconut milk and vinegar drinks.

We introduced ourselves around the table. Next to me was a young man with a sharp undercut and a black hooded sweatshirt, who Lily recognized from their first trip. He had been sitting out in the junction, topless, when they arrived, and he was friendly and welcoming. Beside him was his friend, who had similar hair. It turned out that only about half of the villagers at our table were Mahs, so Lily whispered that we could forget about the red pockets.

The first dish to arrive, after the soup, was a splayed chicken. Its yellow-grey head was placed upright at the top of the plate, beak protruding proudly in the air, stiff yellowish comb erect upon its crown, eyes closed, neck glistening. The rest of its body was cut into neat squares, like a cake, covered in shiny wet skin the colour of cream, sprinkled with chopped spring onions.

Many of the dishes were identical to ones I had seen in Cantonese restaurants in Canada. When we went out for dim sum with relatives in Toronto, my sisters and brother and I used to pick out the miscellaneous meats found in sticky rice and dumplings, hiding the bits in our napkins.

There was no ceremony before the eating of the meal, no speeches or prayers, although the villagers looked to Amanda and me, as hosts, to see if we would open the brandy. If we did, Lily said, it would be taken as a signal that they could too, but we did not touch it.

The meal was so excessive that I did not feel bad about not even attempting to try all the dishes. After the poached chicken came barbecued goose, barbecued pork, fish, green vegetables, lotus root, rice and buns. I ate only rice and green vegetables, and just a tiny piece of the seasonal Qingming goose, but nobody seemed to notice.

'You asked me what I liked best about my first trip to the village, Alice,' Amanda said. 'It was when we all had lunch together in this restaurant on the last day, after finding our home. I felt such an incredible sense of peace.'

At the end of the meal, we went around the tables to give toasts. There were about thirty people, as Lily had guessed, including the village elders and some middle-aged couples and families with young children. Amanda and Matt took Polaroid photographs of the big event and printed them out for everyone. I got some too. For the most part, the photos look like happy family gatherings, although some of the expressions are lukewarm: Auntie Fan, for example, and the woman to whom Amanda had given the red pocket, who decided to come after all. Lily said later that this woman had an unhappy expression throughout the whole meal. Lily tried to comfort her by saying that we genuinely did want to treat everyone to the banquet and were glad to give her a red pocket for missing out the first time. But the woman could not be consoled. I wondered if that was really what was bothering her, and not the sudden conjuring of her lost son.

The bill for the meal was four times the price that Lily had estimated, but she had assumed that she would be able to order the food herself. When we paid the bill, several of the villagers gathered around it. Matt observed that they were probably noting the price that we had paid.

We said our goodbyes, and Lily shuttled rounds of elderly villagers back to Western Peaceful Place. On the drive back to the hotel, she reassured us that the villagers were pleased about the banquet, and that it had not been necessary to give the red pockets after all. She passed on a kind message from Auntie: unlike Uncle Mah, she didn't think that we really needed to build a new house in the village. Still, I felt that we had scraped by having fulfilled the barest minimum of obligation.

9. The Neglected Grave

I might have left the village with just a mild sense of unease, had it not been for the story about the grave. It had a truth that was entirely unexpected. I don't remember sleeping or waking, nor any conversations over breakfast the next day. There is a gap in my memory between the village and the world beyond it, which I cannot fully explain.

Early in the morning, we visited Hill Separated, a village where the railway line used to stop, and where our grandfather wrote that clan records and carvings depicting our ancestry were held in a Buddhist temple. It was our last stop on the Mah village tour. A key-keeper was called in from ploughing the fields to let us into the old clan hall, which was now only used for special occasions. The key-keeper said that he remembered Amanda. How could he forget?

The Mah clan hall was larger than the one in our village, less derelict, and only slightly less disturbing. It was a white rectangular brick building supported by four central pillars, with a tarnished sequence of dragons snaking across the top of its corrugated roof. On the front brick wall, to the left of the central wooden door, there was a faded black and white mural of Mao's face in profile, with his steadfast, unnerving gaze.

Many of the clan halls in China were destroyed during the Cultural Revolution in campaigns to eliminate 'feudal superstition' and to destroy the 'Four Olds': old customs, old culture, old habits and old ideas.[1] Those that remained were converted into communal halls for public torture and beatings. Lily told us this fact again, shuddering at the thought. I was afraid to ask what had happened in her grandma's village.

The hall was stripped bare, like an empty barn, overgrown with weeds, and the only sign of activity was an altar at the back. There were no images of horses as a symbol for the clan, but instead, there were dragons. At the altar was a painting on ceramic tiles of a green dragon snorting grey smoke, surrounded by clouds. It was framed by pink tiles with traditional Chinese characters, echoing the colours of the gateway arch. In Chinese mythology, the green dragon represents the east and the spring, and it symbolizes nature and fertility.

Ironically, the opening of China in the 1980s to 'modern' overseas visitors fostered the restoration of 'feudal' sites and practices. Keen to attract money from wealthy overseas Chinese sojourners, the Chinese government invited donations to rebuild clan halls and ancestral shines.[2] Compelled by old clan loyalties and respect for their ancestors, many sojourners obliged. In other words, the green dragon was a recent addition. The horses had fled.

From Hill Seperated, we set out on the road east, in the direction of Shenzhen. Ying, Lily and I would be travelling to Daya Bay, the site of one of the biggest petrochemical complexes in China. We planned to part ways with Amanda and Matt in Dongguan, where they would continue their travels in China. Ying rode in the front seat, nauseous from the car, and the rest of us squeezed in the back.

In Dongguan, after dropping off Amanda and Matt at their hotel, we stopped for lunch at a sushi restaurant on the way out of the city, a calm, delightfully urban place. We sat on tall chairs by the counter and ordered sushi and tea. Lily leaned back in her chair, her shoulders slackened, and she smiled widely, speaking freely with Ying in Cantonese. It was the first time I'd seen her relax.

There, we discussed the red pockets. Using her sushi plate as a stage, Lily explained the micro-politics of the village drama that had unfolded at the junction, under the banyan tree, utilizing a shell to represent Auntie Fan, a small spoon to represent the elderly woman with the cane and a toothpick to represent Uncle Mah. Ying was fascinated by this episode, as it seemed to confirm all her ideas about life in rural China.

Lily concluded that the whole drama had been orchestrated by Uncle Mah. He had used Auntie Fan to get at the elderly woman with the cane, to try to force us to give everyone red pockets. Lily became very embarrassed and uncomfortable after Amanda gave the elderly woman a red pocket, and frustrated with both Uncle Mah and Auntie Fan, who remained silent and refused to tell the woman the full story, that there was a reason why she was receiving a red pocket and not the others.

Ying suggested that the scheme could have been for Uncle Mah to 'save face' at having been the only one to receive gifts. Lily disagreed: she thought it was just for the money.

Lily also revealed that through all of this, we were not the ones who were at risk, but Lily herself was, because the villagers knew that we didn't understand their tricks, but Lily did and could convey their intentions. They were doing everything they could to get Lily to tell us, in whichever polite ways, to give them red pockets of money. They were very insistent, continually asking her if she had translated their request, and she had to keep saying that she couldn't translate this because it was a cultural difference. On the one hand, she said she felt the pressure to just say 'yes' and ask us to give everyone red pockets. But on the other hand, she had also been warned about the dangers of giving people money, and how it ruins relationships.

'What about the house?' I asked, reminding Lily of the story she told us in Green Vines about the spiritual meanings of ancestral houses, and how Uncle Mah felt sad and guilty that we no longer had a house in the village.

Lily confessed that she now doubted this interpretation. When Uncle Mah said that he was feeling guilty and sad, he was not feeling this at all, she said. Instead, he was using a well-practised technique to ask politely for money. In effect, if we were to build a house, it would be on the village land, and it would be his because he had convinced us to do it. Since we had such a weak link to the village, with no direct relations, she did not believe that Uncle Mah really felt sad about our lack of a house.

I asked Lily whether she thought that, underneath all of this, there was still a sense of kindness on the part of the villagers, that we were welcome in the village, provided we came with gifts. She had, after all, mentioned that Auntie had told her in the car on the way back from the banquet that we didn't really need to build a house.

Lily hesitated before answering. She said that if we understood Chinese, the language as well as the culture, their expectations would not seem greedy. But it would be dangerous for me or Amanda, or any Mahs in our family for that matter, to return to the village again without bringing money. It would not likely be physically dangerous, but we would be given a frosty reception.

I asked if it would be a problem if we never came back again. Would it be perceived as failing to meet an expectation? Lily said frankly, no, they would not care.

As we were getting ready to leave, Lily remembered that there was an unusual story that Uncle Mah had told her, during Amanda's first trip, which she hadn't translated at the time. She found it too difficult to translate. She told the story to Ying in Cantonese, who relayed it to me in English. It was about our great-grandmother's grave.

When Amanda asked after our great-grandmother's tomb, Uncle Mah said that she was buried somewhere in the hills, but he did not know where. Lily said Uncle Mah also commented a great deal during Amanda's first visit about his memory of the story of our great-grandmother's untimely death in the village. He said how it was well known how beautiful our great-grandmother was. Yet he was alluding to something else when he dwelled on her fate, a moral story about familial neglect.

Our great-grandmother died in the village and received her first burial shortly afterwards. But apparently, nobody in our family ever returned to give her a second burial. The ritual of secondary burial is practised in many parts of China. It involves digging up a grave after a set number of years (which varies depending on local customs), picking apart the bones, and then placing the cleaned bones in a special kind of container and reburying them in a tomb upon the hills. Ying said where she comes from, in Macao, they practise secondary burial, too, after a period of seven years. In the Mah village, it is unheard of not to give someone a second burial, at least according to Uncle Mah.

Eventually, the local villagers decided to rebury our great-grandmother themselves, but when they dug up the grave, it had a horrible smell. Uncle Mah said he remembered this smell vividly and associated it with the sad story of the beautiful lady and her abandoned grave.

It wasn't until later, when I pieced together the details, that I saw holes in this account. Our great-grandfather did return to the village ten years after his wife's death, where he also died of an illness. Uncle Mah would have been about three years old when our great-grandfather visited, so it is possible that this is the occasion he mis-remembered, a reburial a few years too late. But details are not the same as truth, and I felt that this was a genuine emotional memory. There was so much within it: disgust, shame, neglect, decay and disrespect. He was saying something with his evocation of smell, his way of contrasting the tale of her beauty with her fate.

I asked Lily once more about the consequences of neglecting an ancestor's grave. She insisted that there were none. But I knew enough about religion to guess otherwise.

PART TWO
Hungry Ghosts

10. Pollution

I never believed in ghosts, not even when I was a child. But somehow, after hearing about her neglected grave, my great-grandmother Woo Doke Yee stayed with me. According to official records, her name was Woo Shee. 'Woo' is a Cantonese transliteration of the Chinese surname Hu/Woo (胡), which means 'non-Han people, especially from central Asia, reckless, outrageous', often translated simply as 'barbarians'.[1] In his memoirs, my grandfather described the Woo clan as 'odd' and 'small', noting their recent migration to Taishan from North-central China.[2] 'Shee' (氏) means wife, or 'from the family of', suppressing a married woman's own identity.

I have only seen one photo of my great-grandmother, taken in 1924 when she was forty-four, and inset posthumously to complete the family portrait in Cranbrook in 1928. She had short hair and a gaunt flat stare.

In Chinese folk religious beliefs, the worlds that separate the living from the dead are porous. The living must feed and care for their deceased ancestors, maintaining a strict and close interaction between the two worlds. Otherwise, neglected ancestors could become vengeful hungry ghosts who unleash illnesses and misfortune on their descendants.[3] Classic Buddhist images of hungry ghosts have bulging stomachs, dishevelled hair and long thin necks, suffering from insatiable neediness. There are many grotesque types of hungry ghost, including those who eat the ashes of cremated bodies; whose food turns to pus, blood or flames; and whose flesh is plagued by insects.[4]

I imagine that hungry ghosts, if they were to exist, would reveal themselves slowly. They might begin inside the body as an unexplained headache, or outside as a creeping algae bloom. Looking back, I think I may have first sensed my great-grandmother's ghost then, on the journey from the Mah village to Daya Bay and back to Guangzhou. Who knows? Maybe it was simply the discovery of an unknown, chaotic part of myself. Or maybe it was the consequence of years of studying environmental devastation, which is a different sort of demon. Whatever it was, I felt something enter my chest on that return journey, a tight and burning sensation. It was the beginning of a kind of unravelling.

At the time, I thought it was just pollution, messing with my senses. Even on a material level, there is something uncanny about pollution. Not everyone experiences it the same way. Ying, who tracked the PM 2.5 readings on her phone every day during our travels in China, could not smell the pollution at all.

On the day before our trip to the Mah village, Ying and I visited two petrochemical villages in Guangzhou. From the old town area of the city where we were staying, we took the metro east to the second last stop on the line. Immediately, as we came out of the metro, the air felt different, noxious. It was worse than the smog in Beijing.

'Oh, that's interesting, how you can smell it,' Ying said, intrigued. 'I can't smell anything. What's it like?'

It was difficult to describe. It was less of a smell than a sensation that penetrated the nose, throat, eyes and skin. I could feel it most acutely at the back of my throat. It had a chemical-sewage-cigarette tang.

The road next to the metro was full of people on bicycles, motorized and manual, in various forms of dress. One person wore oven mitts, some were in suits, others in jeans, and several rode with children strapped to their bodies or baskets.

Ying had arranged a driver for our trip. On her last visit, she had been stranded for over an hour on a narrow road with busy truck traffic, waiting for a taxi. Our driver pulled up in a newish sleek white car, air conditioned, and we drove towards the petrochemical area along winding dirt roads, past thick tropical trees growing low to the ground. Their leaves were covered in dust. Trucks with containers and other heavy loads clattered along the road next to workers on bicycles. After a few minutes, we came to the petrochemical infrastructure and company gates, stopping briefly for roadside photos.

Apart from the palm trees and the signs written in Chinese, the state-owned petrochemical complex resembled other petrochemical landscapes I had seen in the US and Europe – the smokestacks, cylindrical storage tanks and integrated oil refinery.

We were studying the global petrochemical industry, trying to understand the roots of its staggering social and environmental damage. I knew from our research that petrochemicals, which are derived from fossil fuels and used to make plastics and other synthetic materials, are incredibly toxic yet ubiquitous in everyday life.[5] Health effects from exposure to petrochemical pollution include cancer, respiratory illnesses, neurological damage and reproductive disorders. Around the world, petrochemical factories are located near to poor and marginalized communities, reflecting global patterns of environmental injustice. The petrochemical villages of Guangzhou were no exception.

It only took a few minutes to reach the closest village to the petrochemical complex, where we parked and got out of the car. The village was lively. Vendors were selling fruits, vegetables, meat, steamed buns, cooked meals and household items. There were men, women and children walking and cycling through the street, and large trucks drove past frequently, kicking up dust. The hot midday sun and intense smell were overwhelming. While Ying chatted with the steamed bun vendor, I wandered away from the market, along narrow shaded passageways. I saw parked bicycles, workers resting on chairs, and an altar with a small Buddha and sticks of incense in a crumbling brick wall.

Are there things one can observe and understand better – or differently – without language? Vulnerability. Soft bodies, thinly clothed, without protective gear, just a few hardhats, speckled workers' clothes, and children, riding alongside heavy trucks, looming factories, rust and dilapidated structures. I could smell it in my skin.

Most of the people in the village were migrant workers from other regions of China, Ying told me when I met her back on the main road. Before the arrival of the petrochemical industry in the 1970s, the village had been devoted to agriculture, cultivating pineapples, lychees, plums, oranges and Chinese black olives. Now, scarcely anyone from those days was left.

Next, Ying wanted to visit another village a short distance away, one she had been to before. It was slated for demolition, but the villagers did not want to be relocated. There were not many people around. Ying exchanged some small talk with a young woman with a stroller who was walking around the central pond. I bought an ice cream in a shop as an excuse for Ying to talk with the vendor. The ice cream was packaged, so it seemed like a safer choice than the fruit. But when I opened the package, I was not so sure. It was an uneven slab of green tea ice cream and red bean paste sandwiched between wafers, moulded in the shape of a clamshell food container. I tried to eat it, but I could not help thinking that it was petrochemical ice cream.

On the metro back to the old town, I lost my sense of smell. I wondered if that was what had happened to Ying, or to the villagers who claimed not to notice the pollution. In fact, there was a simple explanation for this, I learned later, from an environmental scientist. It was the nitrogen dioxide, which burned out the nerves in your nasal cavities.

So, I carried toxic pollution with me, in my nostrils, even before I got to the Mah village. There was another connection, though, between pollution and the neglected grave. In traditional Chinese burial rituals, a woman's body is believed be polluted, contaminated by birth and death. The *yin* of female flesh needs to be expunged after death, while the *yang* of male bones, associated with purity and cleanliness, needs to be preserved.[6]

There are two different forms of pollution, which are interconnected. One is material, involving the introduction of harmful substances into the environment. This is the kind that I thought I knew well. The other is spiritual, linked to beliefs about impurity and contamination. This is the kind that I did not really want to know.

After stopping for sushi in Dongguan, where we parted ways with Amanda and Matt, we followed the motorway towards Daya Bay, a city on the eastern edge of Shenzhen. Daya Bay is home to a major nuclear plant and one of the largest petrochemical bases in China.

We arrived in the city at dusk. It did not look like an industrial city, but rather like a half-abandoned urban project. For miles and miles, on the approach to Daya Bay, there were stretches of partially built high-rise housing developments, propped up with cranes and scaffolding, amid clusters of grey tower blocks and mounds of dirt.

The area where we were staying was known for foot spas, Lily said, located along the seaside and marketed as a tourist destination. At first, I didn't think it looked touristic at all. The concrete housing blocks were bland, with an air of emptiness, and the shops and restaurants were covered in garish signs. But I recalled visiting seaside amusement towns in Britain and recognized the mood.

The apartment we'd booked was in a middle-class

xiaoqu, a gated community, highly securitized, requiring identity checks and passes to enter. Most of the building was unoccupied, and the air inside was stale. The three-bedroom apartment was fitted out with modern furnishings, including a lounge with a sofa and dining table. From our upper-floor window, we could see the sea and sand in the distance, beyond the houses.

For dinner, Lily and Ying went to a supermarket on the corner of the street and brought back some vegetables to make a salad. They were craving greens after all the meats and salty foods.

Ying investigated the kitchen, a dark narrow room to the side of the lounge. She washed some bowls and cutlery and brought them out to the dining table, along with a chopping board, a knife and some tomatoes.

'Don't look in the fridge,' she warned. 'Or put anything in it.'

I was tasked with chopping the cucumber. I entered the kitchen somewhat reluctantly. All the surfaces were covered with a thin layer of grease. Eventually, I found a long thick knife in one of the drawers and washed it gingerly in the sink.

'Not that one!' Ying exclaimed, glancing up from her tomatoes.

'Why not?' I was confused.

'That one is used for chopping big hunks of meat,' she explained.

As we munched on our vegetables, Ying and Lily looked happy, but I was distracted by thoughts of the meat knife and whatever foul thing lay in the fridge.

Early the next morning, we drove past the petrochemical complex, which bordered the highway into the city. I took blurry photos from the car. It was difficult to get close. We found an urban area next to the highway that overlooked the smokestacks. The concrete buildings were boarded up, and the pavement was cracked with weeds.

In truth, we were all exhausted and lacked a plan of action for this last petrochemical stop in Guangdong. We drove further into the city and stopped at a mall for coffee. Ying saw a poster for a job fair at the mall and went to see if she could find anything out about job opportunities in the petrochemical industry. She came back empty-handed. Most of the people she spoke to did not even know that the petrochemical industry was there. The hot topic that everyone was interested in was housing. Apparently, housing in Daya Bay was booming.

After Daya Bay, we drove to Shenzhen. Ying boarded the ferry to Hong Kong, and Lily dropped me off at the bus station. We both laughed when I paid her with one of the red pockets.

On the airport coach to Guangzhou, I felt my stomach clench. The cucumber had been a bad idea. So much food in China is contaminated, a fact that I had pushed aside.

It occurred to me that rice was another connection between pollution and my ancestors. The Mah village was locked into rice production for food security, but the irony was that the rice was probably contaminated. Despite the continuity of rural life, the village had not escaped the Cultural Revolution, nor was it likely to have escaped toxic pollution.

I thought back to my first research trip to China in November 2015, in the wake of the rice contamination scandal. In 2013, officials in Guangzhou discovered that nearly half of all rice tested in restaurants was contaminated with unsafe levels of cadmium, a human carcinogen that causes kidney damage and other adverse health effects. Several scientific articles followed, outlining the significant public health risks from cadmium-contaminated rice in southern China.[7] I had just started researching the petrochemical industry, and I was in Beijing to attend a conference on environmental health. Outside the conference room, the smog was so thick that we could not even see the buildings across the street. Aside from the air pollution, my main memory of the event was learning that most rice in all parts of China was dangerously contaminated, but this information was a security risk in terms of public disclosure.

After the conference, the delegates went out for a meal in a restaurant. The dishes were beautiful and delicious, but I sensed the hesitation as the rice was passed around.

On a polluted planet, we all eat contaminated food, to a greater or lesser degree, and breathe contaminated air. I felt this most viscerally in China, how inescapable it is, how invasive and how unequal. I also felt the weight of obligation, heavy in my chest, to try to heal the damage.

In Chinese cultural beliefs, my great-grandmother's spirit would have become a hungry ghost long ago. Part of me believed this too. I could imagine her sorrow, but not her wrath. Not yet.

11. Illness

When I opened my suitcase after I got home, I was hit by the overpowering smell of mothballs, acrid and pungent. It must be something else, I realized, carried over from South China. Oddly, I associated it with the smell of Chinese Canadian homes that I had visited as a child. My mom told me the smell came from mothballs stored in cupboards to protect clothes. In fact, the smells were closely related. Mothballs are made from naphthalene or paradichlorobenzene, which are both highly toxic petrochemicals.[1]

For a few weeks, my visit to the Mah village filled my thoughts. I mentioned it to almost anyone who would listen. Uncharacteristically, I even felt compelled to tell the story to an entire dinner party of guests. Gradually, though, the rhythms of everyday life resumed, and the story loosened its hold. I became preoccupied with work, researching toxic pollution in its material rather than spiritual manifestations.

My dad did not seem surprised when I told him about my trip over the phone. 'Mother always said that Father's village was backward,' he said.

It wasn't until spring the next year, in 2019, around the time of Qingming, that my thoughts turned back to the Mah village. There was something about the trip that bothered me, a feeling that I had failed to understand an important aspect. Over the Easter holidays, I took a week off to look back through my notes from the trip and reread my grandfather's memoirs.

I first read my grandfather's memoirs when I was nine years old. He came to visit our family in northern BC, a rare occurrence given the distance from his home in Toronto. He was slight, kindly and hard of hearing. He brought a typewritten draft of his memoirs to share with us. I loved the feel of the stiff typewritten pages, and I was fascinated by this glimpse into our mysterious Chinese identity.

For years, a photocopy of the memoirs lay locked in my family's home safe in my dad's workroom, among other valuable items: our birth certificates; my mom's hand-drawn family tree tracing her roots in Scotland; and a few coins in a plastic folder. From time to time, I would take the memoirs out and skim through the pages, particularly the first chapter, with its intriguing descriptions of the village in China.

Once, when I was a graduate student, I mentioned the memoirs to a professor of Chinese Canadian history, who said that my family should archive them. I reread the memoirs with this idea in mind, but then I cringed at the later chapters on marriage and family.

The trouble was that, really, there were two traumas that haunted my grandfather's memoirs. The first was the death of his mother when he was eight years old. The second was the mental illness of his wife, my grandmother, who suffered for most of their married life from schizophrenia, continually in and out of hospital. The second was not easy to talk about.

My greatest fear, since I was a child, was that I would develop schizophrenia. My grandmother had it, as well as her fourth child, my dad's younger sister, who has lived in a care home since she was fifteen years old. Two of my mom's sisters were also diagnosed with schizophrenia as young adults. My mom told me that schizophrenia runs in families, and it could strike at any time, usually between the ages of fifteen and thirty. Anything could trigger it, especially drugs. There is no cure. The illness involves hallucinations, regular medications, 'episodes', and hospital stays of varying duration. The most terrifying thing, though, was my relatives' failure to distinguish the real from the imagined. Killer bees were taking over the city; Madonna stole my aunt's songs; the dead crows in her apartment were just sleeping.

For years, I watched my mind with hypervigilance, looking for signs. I could imagine how it would happen, the dissolution of my self, tuning out of the world, affixed to another plane.

Now, I was past the age of clinical vulnerability. In revisiting my grandfather's memoirs, I could see the relationships between the two traumas. Both involved the suppression of women's identities.

In 1901, my great-grandfather Mah Gee Su returned from Canada to his clan village in China to find a bride. The matchmakers found it difficult to find him a suitable bride because, at twenty-six, he was considered old, and he was 'small, frail, and an overseas "foreigner"',[2] but eventually they managed to find my great-grandmother Woo Doke Yee, a girl who was 'headstrong and learned, of an odd clan not suitable for the normal peasant farmer'.[3] The matchmakers considered her ideal for an overseas husband because she could read and write, so they could exchange letters.

Their first child Toy Yell, which means 'Wave of Fortune', was born a healthy girl. Happy to have fathered a child in a short time, my great-grandfather returned to the railway town of Cranbrook, BC to run his store in Chinatown, Hep Chong General Merchants, which he established with clan relatives who had prospered during the BC Gold Rush. In 1914, he finally saved enough money to pay the hefty $500 Head Tax imposed on immigrants from China (the equivalent of two years' wages for an immigrant worker) to bring his wife and child over to Canada. They sailed on the *Empress of Russia*, an ocean liner on the Canadian Pacific Steamship Company's passenger route between Canada and Asia, and arrived at the port of Vancouver on 30 May 1914.[4]

My grandfather recalled with pride that his older sister Toy Yell was the first Chinese pupil to attend a public school in Cranbrook. He also wrote that she was a great help in their family's household, caring for him and their other young siblings during the Spanish flu epidemic of 1919. The next year, Toy Yell fell seriously ill and died in hospital. His mother's own deadly illness came a few years later, not long after the incident with the eggs.

One afternoon, around the time my grandfather

started primary school in Cranbrook, his mother discovered a brooding hen in the woodshed beside their rented bungalow on the edge of Chinatown, sitting on a nest of eggs. She gathered the eggs, took them into the kitchen and opened each one carefully. She was delighted to find some with embryos inside, which were considered a delicacy in China and believed to be beneficial to pregnant women. However, her happiness was soon spoiled. My grandfather recalled: 'When Father saw the steamed custard with the embryos on the dinner table, he was very annoyed saying the practice should not be continued in this New Land, as our neighbours would think it barbaric. It was one of the few times that I saw Mother in tears, so Father relented by permitting it one last time. It was not long after that Mother had our youngest baby who died at infancy.'[5]

Throughout his memoirs, my grandfather wrote in an emotionally distant tone, as if he could only observe but not fully understand the feelings of the people around him. He did not cry when his mother died, and he expressed bewilderment at all the wailing and weeping at her funeral. The closest he came to expressing sadness over his mother's death was when their family's housekeeper in Cranbrook left to go back to China: 'I started to cry and bury my head in Auntie's breast because I was distressed that she was leaving us. She had given us the motherly care and attention that I missed since Mother became ill. However, I accepted it stoically as so many things had happened.'[6]

My grandfather mentioned his father's death ten

years later only in passing, as a stressful distraction that affected his high school exam results. After finishing high school, he studied engineering at the University of Alberta in Edmonton and worked in his uncles' restaurant in Cranbrook during vacations. In 1940, my grandfather graduated with distinction, one of the first overseas Chinese to graduate from a Canadian university.[7] He applied to enlist in the war but was rejected because he did not meet the physical requirements of '5 foot 4 inches minimum height'.[8] Due to racial discrimination in BC and Alberta, the only engineering jobs open to my grandfather were in eastern Canada, where hundreds of engineers were being recruited to the aircraft production programme for the war effort. He applied for a job as a trainee airframe fitter in Fort William, Ontario and was hired on the same day.

In 1947, after securing an engineering job at a company in Toronto, my grandfather decided to get married because he felt that he would not be capable of setting up a home on his own. He set out to find a 'suitable mate', conscious that he had limited options given his age and cultural background. Over the Christmas holidays, he attended some Chinese Canadian social gatherings in Toronto and met my grandmother Chu, first at bowling and later at a New Year's party. She was home from teaching in northern Ontario, another job opportunity made possible due to the war. After seeing her a few times again over the summer, my grandfather made up his mind: 'I felt sure that she was the one for my wife because she suited all my needs and desires.' He was impressed by my grandmother's social ease and her experience of working and living independently from her family. He proposed, following Chinese tradition by asking for her father's consent, and Mr Chu accepted, saying my grandmother 'only wanted consent because she was his most loyal and abiding daughter'.[9]

My grandmother had her first mental breakdown not long after their fourth child was born. It happened on the day when my grandfather was due to return to work after the summer vacation. My grandfather found her 'more distraught than usual' that morning, and when he returned for lunch, he found her 'in an agonized state'. She became 'violently incoherent' and 'raving'.[10] At a loss for what to do, my grandfather called the family doctor, who said that she had suffered a mental breakdown and gave her a sedative. My grandmother was taken into a private hospital for psychiatric treatment. That was the beginning of her long-term mental illness. It had probably started years before, when she gave up her own needs and desires as a dutiful daughter and wife.

Maybe that is all that hungry ghosts are, the repetition of trauma in different forms. Or maybe they are more like the caged canaries brought into coal mines to warn of hidden dangers.

After the Easter holidays, I went back to work. I was trying to write an article about toxic petrochemical pollution, but I can no longer remember which article it was. Some people say that their memory gets hazy when they try to recall the time leading up to the Covid-19 pandemic.

What I remember most from that time is lying on the sofa for weeks at home in Coventry, with a bad case of sinusitis. For a few days, I tried writing through the pain, as I desperately wanted to finish my article. But the sinus pressure only intensified, and soon I could not even read, let alone write. My husband had to do all our son's school runs. I closed the curtains to escape the glaring sunlight and sipped bottled Kombucha, waiting for the illness to pass.

2019 was the year of the school climate strikes; I remember that. Everyone was declaring a climate emergency – the city I lived in, the university I worked at, my hometown. Many of us became gripped by an apocalyptic vision: we were going to die, in untold multitudes, by 2050, or by 2100 at the latest.[11] Our deaths would arrive unequally, hitting the poorest and most disadvantaged first. Millions had died already. But soon enough, death would come for us all, and count-less other species too. The sixth mass extinction.

More dramatically still, we could stop the entire calamity in its tracks, if only we stopped burning fossil fuels. Except that we weren't stopping, and most likely wouldn't, not anywhere near fast enough. Emissions kept rising; wildfires set new historic records. We were dangerously close to crossing climate tipping points.[12] It was all or nothing, many concluded: one last shot at redemption or total annihilation. The uncertain in-between space was somehow more difficult to grasp.

After the sinusitis passed, my head still felt cloudy. Through the haze, my research on the petrochemical industry took on a different light. I began to see petrochemicals everywhere: infecting our house in paints, cleaning products and carpets; in smells of burnt plastic wafting up our street from the printing warehouse; in supermarket packaging. Petrochemical pollution is intimately tied to the climate crisis and related existential planetary threats, such as biodiversity loss and marine plastic waste.[13]

The closer I looked, the more disturbing it got. The petrochemical industry has a long track record of deception and violence, profiting from war crimes, marketing products that it knows are harmful to health, squeezing out alternatives, oppressing resistance and lying about it all.[14] It is the largest industrial consumer of fossil fuels and the third largest industrial emitter of greenhouse gases.[15] In spite of environmental pressures, petrochemicals are set to become the biggest driver of oil demand in the energy transition, based on market forecasts for increased global consumption.[16]

Towards the end of the year, as the nights drew in, I started to question the idea of hope. There was something increasingly alienating about the news cycles, especially, ironically, as they focused on issues I had been thinking about: climate catastrophe, pollution, plastic waste. Even sending an email was destroying the planet.

One Sunday in February, we drove to Llandudno, a coastal town in North Wales, for a spontaneous family day trip, my husband's suggestion. It was a crisp and windy day, dry but still battered by floods from the week before. As we entered Llandudno, I admired the juxtapositions, driving past the generic supermarket and bright billboards, with the cliffs, sea and weathered Victorian buildings coming into view. We spent the day walking along the beach, the pier and up a hill, part of the Great Orme, and fortified ourselves with fish and chips, ice cream and hot drinks. Our five-year-old son kept saying how much fun it was, especially climbing 'the mountain'. On the journey back, I felt a reactivated sense of being in the world, as we passed the Runcorn petrochemical facilities near Liverpool. It was a familiar, if toxic, landscape.

Qingming that year, the Chinese Year of the Rat, happened in the middle of lockdown. This time, I did not mark the occasion. Amid all the illness and death, the food stockpiling and home-schooling, I almost forgot about the Mah village, which seemed insignificant in the scheme of things. My writing took on a new tone, more urgent, compulsive. I began to write about toxic pollution and ecological breakdown, finally, with razor-sharp focus. I hardly slept.

But it did not occur to me to ask what possessed me, nor how much it would cost.

12. Ravening

First came the headaches. They would arrive without warning, wrapping around my skull like a boa constrictor, hijacking my focus. I tried taking vitamins, antihistamines and chamomile tea, but I could not identify the source. Next came the palpitations and tremors. I thought they were a reaction to the antihistamines, so I switched to a different kind, but the tremors persisted and the headaches got worse. The most embarrassing thing was the weepiness. It happened when I listened to the radio, when I walked down the aisles of the supermarket, when I spoke with people on Zoom. I would apologize if anyone caught me, saying it was just a weird impact of lockdown and entirely unrelated to my wellbeing.

In fact, I felt very alive. I woke up before dawn every morning to write. I was convinced that I could see something important about the roots of environmental crisis, which barely anyone else could see. If only others could see it, know it, feel it in their bodies, then they would feel compelled to act.

Some days, though, I lost faith. There was a disarming gap between what was happening in the world at large, and in the safety of our home. All around us the world seemed mired in disaster after disaster, yet it could not be touched; we were like turtles, islands, mediated, cracking. The daily deaths from coronavirus, flashing in red news updates, the dire stories about climate breakdown, the mounting volumes of plastic waste, the racist police murders. It was overwhelming, numbing. But my spells of self-doubt did not last long. I redoubled my efforts and worked harder to focus. I let my fixation on ecological catastrophe overtake me, as if it was the only anchor that could keep me from drifting away.

I had nightmares. They were no different from the ones I have always had, just more frequent. In my worst nightmares, I am the villain, and I have committed a terrible crime. They are so violent, so blood-soaked, that they are like watching a horror movie. Their sequence follows a pattern, moving from detached observation towards the dawning realization that I am culpable. When the guilt becomes unbearable, I wake up with vertigo, as if I am falling off a cliff. I switch on the lights and scour my conscience for misdeeds. I find nothing.

Maybe that is why I was so captivated by my great-grandmother's neglected grave. How satisfying, after years of searching, to find something, a sin. Not even a lone one, but a grand, intergenerational one. The idea that every illness, untimely death and disaster is a punishment from hungry ghosts. A divided self, a divided world, a failure to listen, a failure to honour.

After the First World War, my great-grandfather arranged for four of his nephews to come to Canada to study. Apart from my great-grandmother, however, 'none of the women in the family would risk coming to the cold unknown country symbolized by the name Ga-Na-Dye, meaning "Home of Unlimited Vastness"'.[1] Their suspicions about Canada were confirmed when the family returned to China. Both my great-grandmother and her eldest daughter contracted fatal illnesses in the New Land. Aunt Wong said she would never go to such a place.

Yet I doubt that it was a coincidence that my great-grandmother, of the 'barbarian' Woo clan, was the only woman from the family who would agree to go. That was surely part of the bargain.

In a handwritten letter outlining his family tree, my grandfather wrote that the small number of Woo clan members in Taishan were regarded as outsiders by the Cantonese southern clans.[2] They had migrated from North-central China just a few generations before, compared with thirty generations of Mahs in our clan village.[3] Perhaps this was the reason that my grandfather and his siblings were labelled as 'barbaric', and not the strange customs of the New Land.

For her part, my great-grandmother never warmed to Canada. She gave birth to her children at home because she was afraid of the 'devil-looking' nurses at the hospital. During her last days in China, she cried with her mother and sisters in the Woo village about her misfortunes in Gold Mountain. This was curiously consistent with traditional cultural beliefs. In Chinese folk marriage laments, which were sung by women in the days before and after marriage, weddings were seen as a form of death. Brides called their husbands' families 'dead people' and cried that they were dying and needed 'grave clothes'.[4] When married women died, they were buried in their wedding dresses.

Although my great-grandmother received a Christian burial, in addition to a Buddhist one, she never converted to Christianity. Nor did my great-grandfather, for that matter, although my grandfather and his siblings joined the United Church in Cranbrook. Non-Christians would have been classified as 'heathens' in Canada, and I think their Christianity must have been pragmatic, a means of gaining acceptance in a hostile society.[5] It did not carry into the next generation.

When I was growing up in northern BC, there was still a stigma attached to being non-Christian. My hometown had a high number of churches for its population of 5,000 people: Reformed, Anglican, United, Catholic, Baptist, Pentecostal, Free Evangelical, Seventh-day Adventists, Jehovah's Witnesses, Latter-day Saints. My mom used to joke that she was a sinner because the only time she ever went to church, the minister gave her a copy of the Bible with the inscription, 'This book will keep me from sin, or sin will keep me from this book.' My dad never spoke about his views on religion, but something about it seemed to bother him.

One summer, my parents sent me and my sisters to Bible camp because it was the only summer camp available in town, and they told us to just ignore the stuff about God. I tried, but it was difficult. Huge pro-life billboards were displayed along the highway on the edge of town. Some of the kids in my class were taken out of school to prepare for the coming Apocalypse.

In my early teens, I went through a phase of sneaking out to Sunday School at the Pentecostal Church on sleepovers with friends. 'Are you packing church clothes in your overnight bag?' my parents would ask, as if I was smuggling alcohol. The phase didn't last long. I liked the fact that the kids who went to church were nice to other churchgoers, but there was a catch to joining their club. Not only did you have to believe in God, but you also had to denounce the Big Bang.

My discomfort around religion stayed with me. I get nervous every time I encounter a person wearing a clerical collar. I shudder every time I cross the threshold of a church, worried that I am trespassing. Somehow, I feel like the people of the cloth can see right through me, into the depths of my non-believing soul.

Yet, when the world was spiralling out of control, veering into social and ecological collapse, where could one turn to, if not to faith?

My faith, it seemed, was in words. It felt tenuous, barely skimming the surface of reality, but it was something. I devoured books about the deepening climate emergency, the overlapping ecological crises. Just stepping outside your front door, just breathing the air, could be fatal.

I think this was when the ghosts began to take hold, in the long second year of the pandemic, revealing a kind of truth that I already knew in my bones.

13. Climate Breakdown

In times of isolation, you might think that the boundaries between the self and the outside world would harden. But boundaries need practice. Without practice, they weaken, and on re-entering the world, it hits you. There is no filter between what lies beyond and what lies within.

Every summer, on the fifteenth day of the seventh lunar month, the Hungry Ghost festival is celebrated in China. The gates of hell swing open, allowing tortured souls to roam the Earth for a period of two weeks in search of food and entertainment. During the festival, people make offerings of food, incense and burnt paper money to pacify the angry spirits. They avoid certain activities, such as swimming and travelling, for fear of being possessed.[1]

The summer of 2021 in Coventry felt like a pressure cooker, with all the pent-up energy from the pandemic. Parks were unbearably hot and crowded. We stayed indoors through the heatwaves, setting up beach chairs and eating picnics in our living room. For a family holiday, we went camping in North Wales. The roads were clogged, and the service station bins overflowed with litter, but the sand and the waves were majestic. It was a brief respite from the headaches.

That autumn, I offered a new course on sociology

and the climate crisis, back in person after eighteen months online. It was eerie, the social distancing arrows still painted on the pavements, the old food left in office cupboards, the near-empty library. My students seemed eager, almost desperate, to learn. In the first lecture, I announced with some excitement that I would be going to the COP26 Climate Change Conference in Glasgow as part of the university's delegation. I promised to tell them about it. My son said he was proud of me for helping to save the planet.

I don't know what I expected to find, but I was wholly unprepared for that mass Doomsday event, surrounded by more than 40,000 participants.

It is no small thing to realize, not just in mind but in spirit, that the Earth is collapsing. To see the heavy debts that you owe. And to understand, finally, the limits of knowing. For what difference does knowing make? People knew, of course they knew: the facts were all blatantly, dramatically, right in front of us.

At COP26 we were asked to take photos, follow the action, post on social media. Wall-mounted screens displayed the timetables of myriad sessions, like aeroplane departure lists. There were hundreds of reporters, poised with their cameras and notepads. Everything was live-streamed and tweeted instantaneously. I took photos of the tiny talking heads beneath the huge screen heads, the rows of delegates and observers on their phones.

A pink neon artwork in the hall read: 'Hurry up please it's time'. A group performed a skit in the hall, with men dressed as bankers, symbolizing rich countries, holding a giant cheque made out to developing countries for 'empty promises only'.

The Pavilion of national exhibits resembled a futuristic miniature city, words and images streaming disaster scenarios and technological solutions. Delegates crammed to hear talks in the divided sections, many wearing headsets, plugged into hybrid realities.

Climate action was urgent, of life-and-death importance, and people's suffering was laid bare in two-minute testimonies. *We have been here before; our grandchildren will not forgive us; it is a death sentence; prove us wrong.* Those voices will haunt me forever, the desperate pleas and seething indignation, the grief swelling in those airless halls.

It was difficult to find anywhere to rest. People sat perched against walls in the hallways. Negative Covid tests and facemasks were compulsory, but social distancing was impossible. The on-site convenience shop sold out of painkillers.

On the penultimate day, as the negotiations intensified, I sat on the top floor of the circular Action Zone, overlooking the River Clyde, glued to the online portal and its reel of briefings. When I finally resurfaced, something gave way. I knew it was over. Everything felt flat, beyond words. I bought a cup of coffee on the ground floor, sat at a table and cried.

There was no chance of averting catastrophe. That was where the hopeful politicians and activists had it wrong. This was the course we were on.

The next morning, I rode the train back to Coventry,

watching the final hours on my laptop, still unable to look away. While I passed the green fells of the Lake District, hundreds of civil society observers staged a walkout of COP 26 to join activists on the streets, carrying blood-red ribbons to symbolize the red lines that the negotiations had crossed.[2]

Outside the newly renovated Coventry train station, I paused at the City of Culture information booth to glance at the brochures. Once known as the UK's 'motor city', Coventry was the UK City of Culture in 2021, a title awarded every four years to a post-industrial city in need of regeneration. Coventry's motorcar heritage featured prominently in its year of cultural events, a fact that I knew but which suddenly felt jarring. Every year, Coventry celebrates MotoFest, where the city's ring road is taken over for a weekend by souped-up race cars, the air blackens with exhaust, and engines rev and rumble all day. This year was the biggest MotoFest yet.

At home, my son hugged me and asked how the conference was. I tried to hold back my tears.

'It's a good thing you weren't planning a visit to Canada,' my dad told me over a video call that weekend.

'It's end times here,' my mom added. She started using this phrase during the pandemic, in a half-serious way. The island was facing stormy weather, and they were worried about the news from the mainland.

On 13 November, the day the Glasgow Climate Pact was agreed, an 'atmospheric river' made landfall on the west coast of British Columbia, and meteorologists warned of severe rainstorms and flood risks across the lower mainland. Nicknamed the 'Pineapple Express', this type of atmospheric river carries water vapour from the tropical Pacific near Hawaii to the west coast of North America, travelling along narrow 'rivers in the sky', resulting in extreme rainfall, flooding and mudslides. By 15 November, the city of Abbotsford, BC and several neighbouring communities in the Sumas Prairie farmlands had declared states of emergency and issued evacuation alerts.

Flooding and landslides in the region caused significant damage to highways and railways, cutting off access to the port of Vancouver. There were travel disruptions and food shortages in grocery stores. Farmers desperately tried to rescue their cows, pigs and chickens from the rising waters. Five people died in landslides, 3,300 people lost their homes, and 640,000 farm animals died from drowning, building collapses, starvation or electrocution.[3]

The disastrous floods followed in the wake of a wildfire-related state of emergency in BC earlier that year, when more than 1,600 wildfires burned nearly 8,700 square kilometres of land. One of the worst wildfires destroyed the village of Lytton, making international headlines. The fire started on 30 June, the day after Lytton recorded the highest ever temperature in Canada (49.6°C). Most of the village burned to the ground, and thousands of people were evacuated from the village and the neighbouring Lytton First Nation reserves.[4]

My parents were rattled by this news. In the mid-1970s, they spent a few days visiting Lytton, when they were looking for a place to start a family. They nearly moved to Castlegar, another picturesque town in southern BC, not far from Cranbrook, but they decided to move north instead.

Inhabited for thousands of years by the Nlaka'pamux people, the Lytton area is located at the confluence of the Thompson and Fraser rivers. As a former Gold Rush and railway town, Lytton once had a significant Chinese population. Among the many losses in the wildfires was the Lytton Chinese Canadian History Museum, which was built on the historic site of a demolished Chinese temple. Nearly 1,600 artefacts detailing the lives of Chinese miners, railway workers, merchants and farmers in the BC interior were destroyed.[5]

Several media reports drew connections between the floods and wildfires. Burnt soils are water-repellent, leading to increased runoff and risk of landslides. The hills next to Sumas Prairie blazed throughout July.[6]

Many reports also pointed to another dimension: the dangers of ignoring traditional land uses. One hundred years ago, the Sumas Prairie was a large shallow lake on the Traditional Territory of the Semá:th people, a rich wetland filled with fish and waterfowl. Sumas Lake would rise and fall with the seasonal floods of the Fraser River, frustrating white settler farmers along its shores. In the 1920s, the BC government decided to drain the lake to control the flooding and create more lucrative farmland. The Sumas Prairie, now covered with dairy and chicken farms, sits below sea level. In 2013, the Sumas First Nation began working on a land claim to seek compensation for the loss of Sumas Lake, a process that could take decades.[7]

This story felt personal, even though I've never lived in that part of the province.

The railway town I come from was built on a swamp in a mountain river valley on the unceded land of the Wet'suwet'en people, a thirteen-hour drive northeast of Vancouver. It was founded in 1913 as the divisional headquarters of the Grand Trunk Pacific Railway and named after the chairman of its board of directors, Sir Alfred Smithers. When I was growing up, the main local history book was called *Smithers: From Swamp to Village*, a story of white settler domination over nature and Indigenous land.[8] Signs of the town's swamp history would resurface in the springtime when the snow melted and the school playing fields turned into vast, stinking ponds. My parents retired to Vancouver Island more than a decade ago, and I have not been back to Smithers since. The town is often under threat of evacuation due to wildfires and flooding.

Many inhabited places in the world have a story like this, a suppressed identity waiting to be released. In Coventry, there is an eight-mile stretch of hidden river that flows under the city centre. Most residents are unaware of its existence. In the 1960s, the River Sherbourne was diverted under the city through a pipe to support urban development, opening out at the industrial and suburban fringes.[9] If you listen closely, you can hear the river trickling through the drainpipes, or, if you know where to look, find a short passage of water flowing beside a lane.

One of the City of Culture events was timed to coincide with COP26, a sound exhibition called 'Listening to the Anthropocene' at Coventry Cathedral. I took my son to it one weekend. Along the side of the main cathedral hall, speakers piped out sounds of the Sherbourne, recorded by London-based sound artist Kate Carr, who spent several weeks following the elusive river. The faint sploshing noises mixed with whirs of recorded traffic were scarcely audible with all the footsteps and voices in the cathedral. I don't think many of the visitors even knew that the exhibition was on; the information panels were easy to miss. Still, there was something intimate about listening to the river in this space. It required tuning in to another register, beneath the surface. And I realized, to my surprise, that I no longer felt like I was an intruder in this church. Never mind that what I was tuning in to, at last, were the hungry ghosts escaped from hell.

14. Inferno

At the start of winter, the Coventry bin strikes began. The garbage piled up, and the whole city began to smell. Among the crocuses, which arrived early that year, we spotted the first rat in our garden, by the back fence next to the railway line, its nose in a bucket of rainwater. I have always liked rats. I take it as a good omen if one peers out from a bush or a crack in the pavement. An encounter with a rat in the city suggests that I am at peace, for a moment, with the world. It is different, though, when a rat comes close to your home and brings its mischief.

For months after the climate conference, I felt the pull of the Abyss. I named it to laugh at it, diminish its power. It comes every winter as the days draw in and slowly retreats in the spring. Usually it is gentle, a sadness that hums throughout everyday life. But this time, it took on a new shape, fierce and unpredictable.

'People will die from heat exposure, within hours, just from stepping outside!' I raged on the chat during an online meeting at work. Two thumbs up, one heart emoji. Yes, we should do something more about limiting air travel, my colleagues agreed, but we shouldn't be too excessive. My eyes welled up, and suddenly they were more conciliatory, which infuriated me even more. It was their mentality that upset me, not the air travel, carrying on as usual, pretending that everything would be okay.

Of course, in those times, we were all reeling from our own losses, great and small. I suffered only a small one, no bigger than the size of a heartbeat, though I never gave her a proper burial.

The hungry ghosts that roam the Earth include all angry spirits, not only dead relations. Some of the most dangerous ghosts are the ones who died of drowning, who grab at people when they enter bodies of water. The ghosts who died of suicide are also malevolent, seeking vengeance against their relatives through death.[1]

In the aftermath of natural disasters in China, people would get particularly anxious about the need to pacify the wrath of those who had died. Following an outbreak of bubonic plague in Guangzhou in 1894, when between 200 and 500 people died every day, local elites held a ritual assembly of 10,000 people to make offerings to the departed masses. During the Mao years, the Qing-ming and Hungry Ghost festivals were banned as folk superstitions to be cast aside. But people practised these rituals anyway, especially during the Great Famine.[2] Through the fires, floods and pandemic, I felt this anxiety too, but had no ritual to keep it at bay.

In the third week of February 2022, Russia invaded Ukraine. The news was everywhere, awful, incomprehensible. It was too much to let in. I had nightmares about flooding and nuclear war.

When stories of death get into my mind, they get stuck. There are images that have lodged there for decades, gruesome, senseless, that I have worked very hard to erase. When I wait for a bus, I pull my head back as the bus approaches, so it does not get knocked in by the wing mirror. That happened to a student in my art class in the late 1990s.

Objects took on aggressive qualities. Knives left on countertops, garden implements outside, seemed threatening, and I had to put them away.

When the panic attacks started, I finally reached out for some help.

'Do you tend to overthink things?' my therapist asked.

'Define overthinking,' I said.

After a few weeks, I gave up. My 'intrusive' thoughts about the climate crisis were not distortions; they were real.

Come spring, my chest had settled into an ever-present thrum. Over the holidays, we went camping on the Isle of Arran in Scotland. Our son spent hours combing through rocks and shells along the beach. The winds were favourable, so we took the ferry to the Holy Isle, which is owned by a Tibetan Buddhist community. Their centre was still closed due to coronavirus, but the long-term meditation retreats were running. The ferry captain said there were a few women staying on the isle who had started their three-year retreats before the pandemic. We hiked up the steep rocky path to the mountain summit past heather and quaking grass. Looking out across the ocean, we thought we spotted a whale but, in the binoculars, it was a nuclear submarine.

As we hurried to catch the ferry back, we passed the Eriskay ponies, a rare breed of crofters' pony with ancient Celtic and Norse origins in the Western Isles of Scotland.[3] I thought about the loss of ancestral lands, species and knowledge. Although it felt raw, it had been happening for millennia. My Taishanese ancestors knew how to tend rice fields and keep tombs dry upon the hills, yet they also lived through ecological crisis. They migrated overseas to escape droughts, famines, epidemics and conflict. That was part of their lost history too.

In Chinese folk beliefs, the hungry ghosts of neglected ancestors underlie such disasters. But what unleashes the vengeance of hungry ghosts? From what I have read, it is not through sin, at least not like in Christianity. It is through unbearable suffering, which ruptures the cycle of obligations between the living and the dead. There is no possibility of escape. Most spirits pass into the underworld after death and need to receive constant food and 'hell money' from their relatives. Hell is not even the worst place. Those who lose their bodies in death are denied entry to hell, forced to wander endlessly in limbo, the most fearsome of the hungry ghosts.[4]

Admiring the spare, windswept hills and the rhythmic hum of the ocean, I could not decide whether it was comforting or not, the relentlessness of this cycle.

Back in Coventry, the bin strikes dragged on. The rats scampered between the terrace gardens through gaps in the fences, raiding the birdfeeders. Around the country, workers who had been deemed essential throughout the pandemic were striking over pay and working conditions. The nurses went out on strike for the first time in more than a century.

I took a particular relish in 'No-mow May' as an excuse to let our garden grow wild. My mom used to mow the lawn compulsively, every other day. I sent her a photo of our two-foot-tall grass.

In early June, we received a text from our neighbour's landlord: 'When are you going to cut the hedge? I asked you about this weeks ago. You don't want to be "neighbours from hell". ☺'

We responded that it would not be anytime soon, because of the nesting birds.

One midsummer evening, I sat at the kitchen table and contemplated the state of our garden. We were going to have to do something about it. Suddenly, I heard a heavy clack on the floor beside me, in the base of the old fireplace. Sometimes when the wind picked up, a clump of soot would drop and scatter on the floor. But this felt more substantial. I glanced over and let out a shriek. Two tiny bird feet stuck into the air, out of a bloody, feathered lump.

My husband was tasked with removing the half-bird body. He suspected the magpie butcher he saw flying angrily from our roof.

'Shouldn't we bury it?' our son worried. The bin lid shut. It was just the feet, not the whole bird, we tried to explain.

During the first lockdown, my husband built a raised

bed with our son, and they planted radishes, beetroot, courgettes, cucumbers and lettuce. The lettuce bolted, but the cucumbers were a success, and we used some of the beetroot for a chocolate birthday cake when the shops were out of flour. The next year, we planted wildflowers instead.

This summer, we tried vegetables again, and the rats ate all our beetroot. The bin strikes ended, but the Abyss refused to leave.

15. Chill

The closest I got to touching my great-grandmother's wrath was during my last year in Coventry. I hope never to get that close again.

In the summer of 2022, I chose to believe that travel was safe and went to a social sciences conference in Amsterdam, my first face-to-face one since before the pandemic. Crammed in the Eurostar lounge in London St Pancras with thousands of travellers in the middle of a heatwave, I knew it was probably a mistake. The conference hotel was a former women's psychiatric hospital, in the Oosterpark, not far from the university. It had grand, austere staircases and floor-to-ceiling white curtains draped along the corridor walls. My room was on the third floor, modern and capacious yet bleak.

On the evening of my arrival, smoke drifted in through the windows. I guessed it was from the barbecues that people were enjoying outside in the park. It grew heavier and began to smell like burnt plastic. At around nine o'clock, an emergency alert shrieked on my phone. A fire had broken out on a scrap metal heap at a recycling company on the outskirts of the city. We were instructed to close windows, turn off ventilation and stay indoors.

The train journey back was even busier, and hotter. In London, the underground was closed due to a transport strike. The streets were sweltering and heaving, like I had never seen before, all the subterranean travellers thrown up onto the surface.

A week later, I tested positive for Covid, which I had been fortunate to avoid so far. I was grateful that it was relatively mild, and that nobody else in our house got it, although it lingered for months. After the aches subsided, I found that they could be reactivated through certain triggers. It was as though I had grown hackles, like a cat, that raised on the slightest provocation.

My coffee tasted like soil; the surface of my skin vibrated. Work, which was normally my refuge, became exhausting, uncontrollable. I drew the short straw that year and had to take on new responsibilities in management. Immediately, I felt a rebelliousness inside that I didn't know how to channel. Fighting the machine only to be told to be realistic. Unable to speak without fear of losing control. The machine was insidious, seeking to incorporate different selves, bit by bit, until all the parts aligned. In the worst moments, it felt like being lacerated with spikes and vines.

I cut my hair short and wore thick black eyeliner, like I did as a teenager.

One Sunday in mid-November, we went for a family walk from the university to the surrounding countryside. When it was built in the 1960s, the University of Warwick was like a space station that had landed in the fields. It spread out along the banks of the River Avon, between meadows, woods and wetlands. At lunch, I often walked to the river to watch the herons and moorhens.

The sun glowed white under the thickening clouds, as we followed the path through green fields and woods. Around a bend, we came to rows of metal fences, stretching down a hill into a vast expanse of red soil churning below.

'Trespassers keep out,' our son read the sign. 'This land is in possession of HS2. Trespassers will be subject to criminal proceedings . . . What is HS2?'

I told him about the new high-speed railway that they were building between the West Midlands and London, how it threatened more than a hundred ancient woodlands. But he was already upset, and I held back from saying more.

It was the first time we had witnessed the wreckage up close, the hulking bulldozers, the fenced-off trees awaiting their slaughter.

Bits of the Earth were breaking off. Swallowed in flames, eroded, sliced. Those in safety were aware of it, lapping at the edges of their worlds, but until it approached, what was there to do? Panic and protest; or continue as normal, ants, marching, synchronicity disturbed.

That day, out in the mangled woods, I knew that I wanted to escape. For years, we had dreamed of moving to Scotland, where my husband comes from. Now, it felt urgent. It is not easy to leave a place you call home, but I had done it before. I got out of my hometown, which was never really a choice, and then out of BC, Ontario, Canada. Everywhere I went, I was seeking new adventures, but I was also propelled by claustrophobia. At eighteen, when I moved to Vancouver, I often ran into people from my hometown, who seemed to frequent the same parts of the city, the outdoor stores, cafés and forest trails. I tried my best to avoid them. They reminded me of the former self I had shed.

My ancestors, too, were those who escaped. They followed the lure of gold in distant lands, became entangled with settler colonial expansion. There are consequences to shedding one place and entering another, making a deal with the white devil instead of the hungry ghosts.

I imagined meeting my great-grandmother. I could only picture her in black, with the hollow pallor from that photo, and trembling hands. She carried her pain with her, of lost children, adrift in the unwelcoming New Land. Already I was as old as she was when she died.

I felt a chill all over my body. My hackles were raising again, a tuning fork for what lay beneath.

We tried to warn you, she said. There is no escape. *We have been here before. Our grandchildren will never forgive us. It is a death sentence. Prove us wrong.*

It was only then that I realized that, with a contaminated inheritance, anger works both ways.

16. Bones of Gold Mountain

I know what not to do with anger: bury it deep inside. But I do it anyway. For most of my life, I did not even know it was there. I thought anger was an irrational emotion, associated with shouting and swearing. Sometimes, at most, I washed the dishes too loudly. If something really bothered me, I became silent until it passed. I did not know that such repression is unhealthy, leading to autoimmune disorders, where the body eats away at itself.[1]

The hungry ghosts taught me about anger, burning white hot. I could feel it all around me, borrow it briefly, yet never fully own it. Once it surfaces, I bury it again.

Maybe I inherited this trait from my female ancestors, who were forced to swallow their grief. But I suspect that I got it more from the male clan line: stoic; compulsively driven.

On the wall in my dad's workroom was a picture of two horses in bronze relief, galloping, manes swirling. I used to think our surname had the same meaning as the horse in the Chinese zodiac, suggesting that we are friendly, energetic and cheerful. In fact, it signifies cavalry horsemen, the opposite of wild horses. It is said to come from 'Ma Fu', which means 'Tamer of Horses', an honorific title given to a prince of the state of Zhao during the Warring States period in China (475–221 BCE) for military victories.[2]

How disappointing to find out that you are descended from the victors, especially when you were always told that you came from the oppressed.

The first Chinese migrants to Canada faced many forms of oppression: labour exploitation; racist immigration policies; violent attacks; and everyday discrimination. In 2006, the Prime Minister of Canada offered a formal apology to Chinese Canadians for the Chinese Head Tax (1885–1923, a tax on each Chinese person entering Canada) and the Chinese Exclusion Act (1923–47, a law banning most forms of Chinese immigration), acknowledging that these 'malicious measures, aimed solely at the Chinese, were implemented with deliberation by the Canadian state'.[3]

Four of my great-grandparents paid the Head Tax, and the subsequent generation fought hard to gain citizenship rights. I am indebted to them all. Yet, I cannot help picking at scars.

Early Chinese migration to Gold Mountain was rooted in the nineteenth-century Gold Rush, which pillaged Indigenous lands. The earliest racial conflicts were over the spoils. White workers were hostile towards Chinese miners like my great-grandfather, who trekked for days through rough mountains to the goldfields of Wild Horse Creek in BC in the 1890s. Chinese migrants were only permitted to rework the diggings of abandoned gold claims because they could not stake their own claims as non-citizens. Nonetheless, as my grandfather recalled, 'some made as much as ten thousand dollars, a fabulous amount at that time, enough to retire to China'.[4]

My great-grandfather prospered during the Gold Rush. Later, he avoided the heavy labour of building the railroads, and instead set up business as a merchant in Chinatown with clan relatives. He was one of very few Chinese men in those times who was wealthy enough to bring his wife and family over from China. Despite being low in the hierarchy of settler colonialism, they were among the most privileged Chinese in Gold Mountain.

In histories of survival through the generations, I guess it is inevitably more common to have descended from people who thrived, in one way or another. Through the years of anti-Chinese immigration policies, the China-towns in Canada were populated primarily by men, who left their families in China to take backbreaking and poorly paid jobs. Many left no descendants. The plight of Chinese railway labourers is particularly harrowing. They had a special clause in their contracts, stipulating that if they died, their remains would be shipped back to China. Even then, most of their bones never made it back.[5]

Both my great-grandparents returned to die in the Mah village. Their bodies may not have been properly buried, and their tombs may have been left unswept, but they made it back. I wonder now if that makes any difference: in the realm of hungry ghosts, is there a hierarchy of ancestral neglect?

In the lucky Year of the Rabbit, my husband and I found new jobs in Glasgow and made plans to move. The most difficult thing about moving, for our son, was the loss of our garden. He made intricate pencil drawings of the crocuses and insisted on planting vegetables, even though we would not stay long enough to harvest them.

I booked flights to visit BC with our son that summer to use the last of my annual leave. I called my dad to see if I could convince him to join us for a short trip to Cranbrook. We could walk through the former streets of Chinatown, I suggested. It could be fun.

'No, thanks,' my dad said. He had already been to Cranbrook, many years ago. 'There is nothing to see there. If anything, I would rather visit the village in China.'

'Really?' I said, getting excited. 'When can we go?'

'Oh . . .' he paused. 'Well, not until I have saved up a huge wad of cash.'

My dad has a dry sense of humour, and it is difficult to tell when he is teasing me. But then he surprised me by turning to a serious subject: his family's relationship with money, which he had never mentioned before. He said that his parents often argued about money, which was tight, and about whose family was more respectable.

There was a running joke between his parents about the question of their fathers' 'sidelines'. It was a 'romantic question', my dad explained. How had his two grandfathers managed to make so much money, while on paper they were both relatively humble? In particular, he wondered about his mother's side of the family. His mother was one of eight children, who each became professionals. Even his mother, despite being one of the daughters, had a teacher's degree. Each daughter married well, and their weddings were well catered for. How did his grandfather manage to afford all of this, as the owner of a modest laundry? Why, at the age of sixty-five, was he still riding around Toronto on his bicycle delivering baskets? What was he really carrying?

I smiled at this hint of aspersion, the guilty pleasure of speculation without evidence. Later, looking through newspaper archives, I could find no evidence of sidelines. On the contrary, my great-grandfather Mah (business name Hep Chong) was featured in an article in *The Cranbrook Herald* in October 1915, as a 'Chinese Example of Patriotism'. He paid a war tax of $27.00 on imported Chinese wine, which he was entitled to have returned, but: 'no, he did not want it. Let it go to the war, to the Patriotic Fund, to the Red Cross, for the wounded men coming back from the war, said he.' He was commended as 'a Chinese gentleman . . . a good citizen, a man worth knowing, and a splendid example for others to follow'.[6]

This was in sharp contrast to other descriptions of Chinese people in local newspapers at the time, which spoke of the Chinese as 'the most servile of races . . . a heathen willing to work for barely enough to sustain life';[7] with 'their noiseless, shadowy, mysterious ways something of a problem';[8] and cited a pithy quote: 'For ways that are dark and for tricks that are vain the heathen Chinese is peculiar.'[9]

My grandfather's memoirs yielded more, but nothing that was not typical for those times. There was the mysterious package filled with opium that arrived at his father's store, sent by an 'unscrupulous enterpriser',[10] resulting in a lengthy police investigation. Eventually, the case was dropped, and they took greater care with packages after that. The store was also a hub for social gambling. The Reverend from the United Church came to the store to ask them to stop because it was a 'moral sin'. However, my great-grandfather 'allowed and often participated in social gambling' because it was consistent with his stoic philosophy of 'So Be It' (Hai Kuo), a Chinese proverb.[11] The city authorities often raided the social club next door for playing Fan-Tan, a gambling game of chance played for 2,000 years in China, but my grandfather said they tolerated 'social gambling'.[12]

The most unsettling descriptions of illicit activities in the memoirs were of the brothels. My grandfather devoted several paragraphs to discussing various 'cathouses' and 'social houses', with a combination of adult and childlike fascination. His uncle delivered laundry to a brothel in a farmhouse a mile out of town, which catered for white clientele. My grandfather sometimes tagged along for the ride, and the madam gave him fruit and cookies to eat while he waited in the car. The Chinese had 'their own outlet' in the social houses next to Chinatown run by Japanese and African American women 'to meet the needs of the lonely unattached Chinese man'.[13]

Rereading these vignettes of life in Chinatown in the depressed years after the Gold Rush, I felt a strange surge of compassion. The Chinese sojourners in Gold Mountain sought escape but could never seem to find it. Chinatown was filled with needs that knew no end.

The Canadian physician Gabor Maté compares the

Buddhist realm of hungry ghosts to addiction, 'where we constantly seek something outside ourselves to curb an insatiable yearning for relief or fulfilment'. [14] Maté worked as a doctor for many years with drug addicts on Vancouver's Downtown East Side, and he came to understand their addiction as an attempt 'to escape the Hell Realm of overwhelming fear, rage and despair'. [15] He argues that addiction manifests in many different forms, beyond drugs and alcohol, including compulsive gambling, sex, eating, shopping, extreme sports, Internet use and work, and that it is all rooted in lived experiences of trauma. So too, he says, are many illnesses, which emerge when the yearnings are suppressed.[16]

My grandfather wrote about his ailing health in the last decade of his working life, his worsening allergies, hypertension, diabetes, stomach cramps and breathless angina, which flared up with the regular hospital confinements of his wife and daughter for their schizophrenic episodes. He had to take extended sick leave and a disability allowance, before stopping work altogether. After he retired in 1982, he travelled around Canada visiting relatives, and wrote his memoirs. He died of a heart attack in 1989, at the age of seventy-two, which seemed old when I was a child but seems too young now. I remember my dad flying to Toronto for the funeral, how stricken he looked. My dad says that my grandfather lived a good life and achieved what he wanted. I am sure that he did. There is a difference, though, between wants and needs.

17. Rituals

The most exhausting thing about the ghosts was their refusal to leave. I noticed them, felt them, heard them, but still, it was not enough. It made no difference whether I believed in them or not. Once I thought they had gone quiet, they started to scream again.

On Qingming, five years after my trip to the Mah village, I was in Glasgow with my son over the Easter holidays, getting a feel for the city before our move. We went to the Science Centre that morning. Somehow, I forgot it was a place I had been to before.

We took the local train to Exhibition Centre station from Glasgow Central. Right away, I recognized the long red covered walkway coming out of the station, which looked strange now it was so empty, coated with green and black mould. I could not help pointing out the mould to my son, but then I regretted adding to his worries. We held our breath and picked up our pace.

The walkway opened out onto the Scottish Event Campus, and a green sign directed us along a concrete path. The campus was peaceful without all the people and security barriers. It had been folded back to its original state, ready for the next crowds.

Beyond the SEC Armadillo, built in the 1990s to resemble the interlocking hulls of a ship, we came to a lone towering crane by the River Clyde and stopped to appreciate it for a few moments. Up close, it had more presence than I remembered, almost stubborn in its stance.

The Clyde was calm, the sky overcast and threatening to rain. We followed the footbridge over to the south side towards the Science Centre. This bridge had been reserved for VIPs as a fast-track entrance to the Blue Zone, the official negotiation space of COP26. The rest of us entered through heavily policed metal turnstiles along the main road to the east, weaving past people wearing ghoulish costumes and waving placards about death.

As soon as we entered the Science Centre, I recognized the place. It was the Green Zone, the dedicated space for public engagement at the COP. I went there one afternoon with three other members of my university's delegation, a life scientist, an economist and a student, but we'd approached it from the opposite side. On our walk from the Blue to the Green Zone, we passed a group of people singing in rueful chorus on the verge of the road, wearing flowing garments. Their voices were soft and angelic. Part of me wanted to join them, to experience whatever catharsis they were feeling. In that moment, it seemed like the world was literally ending.

The Green Zone was much the same as the Blue Zone, with shorter queues. We had our photo taken at the entrance in front of the flowery 'Welcome to COP26' sign.

My son loved the Science Centre, especially the optical illusions. I enjoyed it too, but I kept seeing traces of its former use. On the second floor, there was an exhibition about renewable energy. We took a break in the futuristic chair pods along the wall, which each had individual electronic tablets, like aeroplane seats, featuring press releases and articles related to COP26.

'Didn't they invent nuclear fusion already?' my son asked as he scrolled through the displays.

'Yes,' I said and smiled at him, recalling the recent breakthrough. 'This exhibition was created before.'

On the train back from Glasgow, watching the moving greenery shrouded in mist and low clouds, I thought of the drive to the Mah village on the day of Qingming. So much had changed in five years. On the surface, the British countryside seemed gentler than the ravaged hills of Taishan, although I knew there was violence beneath it too.

Perhaps the most famous part of Coventry is the cathedral, not the new one built in 1951 after the Second World War, but the bombed-out ruins of the one before, which are preserved across the lane. You can walk among the ruins, which are surrounded by four walls, vaulted arches and open sky. In the middle is the stump of a spiral staircase. A sign on the wall says that the burning metal frame inside the cathedral walls was what caused the building to collapse, as it twisted in the flames after being hit by incendiary bombs. Children today like to play among the worn stones, hiding in corners, climbing the staircase.

Leaving Coventry was almost more difficult than staying. *How can you leave us? Aren't we good enough?* Even more painful than the collegial guilt was the sadness in my friends' smiles, and the months of lingering in everyday routines. The rituals of leaving resembled those of death: awkward silences; unwieldy emotions.

Inexplicably, in my last year in Coventry, five of our retired professors died, one after another, from different illnesses. They were from the same generation of scholars, each treasured and cherished in their own unique ways, and each loss was unexpected and heart-rending. I had to make the announcements.

Was it an occupational hazard that I never knew about, I began to wonder, or a delayed effect of the pandemic on this generation of sociologists, ageing in fractured times?

Everywhere I looked, I was reminded of death. I shut the news out completely. Surprisingly, I found comfort in reading books about death rituals in China: the number of years – five, seven, or ten – between burial and 'secondary burial', where the bones are separated from the flesh; the preparation of the soul tablet, where the name of the deceased is written on a tablet and stored in a domestic altar in their household; and the origins of 'ancestor worship', which is practised across social classes and religions in China, and influenced by a remarkable fusion of Confucian, Indigenous, Buddhist and Taoist beliefs.[1] It made me feel closer to my ancestors.

I began to avoid things in fours, like the number of

slices in fruits and vegetables when preparing snacks and meals. Four is an unlucky number in China because the word for four, *si*, sounds like the word for death. It is impossible to avoid the number four. There are four seasons; four legs of a table, bed, desk and chair; four corners of compass, door, picture and house; I am one of four siblings. But I could not bring myself to quarter an apple without dividing it again.

Growing up, I never paid much attention to superstitions, nor did I think about where they came from. 'Step on a crack, you'll break your mother's back.' 'Don't put new shoes on the table.' 'Touch wood.' These are common British and Irish folk superstitions for avoiding death and misfortune. Cracks in the pavement represent portals to the underworld, and stepping on a crack invites an evil spirit to cause harm. Putting new shoes on the table is bad luck, linked to death, illness and contamination. And people touch wood to avoid tempting fate, seeking protection through connection with trees.[2]

Of course, you cannot go through life without stepping on cracks. The table is also a convenient place to unpack a box of new shoes. Touching wood, however, is different. It happens after, not before, a misstep, and it engages with protective rather than harmful spirits. I have seen many people knock on wood, then pretend it is a joke to mask their compulsion. It is not just me.

Even among Western doctors and surgeons, there is a widely held superstition about the *q*-word – 'quiet' – which should never be spoken during a hospital shift.

Several research papers have examined whether there is a correlation between saying the *q*-word and higher incidents of medical emergencies.[3] There does not seem to be any correlation, but this misses the point. When we are surrounded by calamity and uncertainty, this is where the mind goes.

Eight is one of the luckiest numbers in China. It is pronounced *ba*, which sounds like the word for wealth and prosperity. For Buddhists, eight is also auspicious because of the Noble Eightfold Path towards liberation from the cycle of suffering: right understanding, right thought, right speech, right action, right livelihood, right effort, right mindfulness and right concentration.

How appealing, the thought of breaking free from the cycle.

My guiltiest act in leaving was the betrayal of the ants. In the dry summer heat, they liked to come in through a tiny hole in the back wall, under the drainpipe, leaving little heaps of sand under the skirting board. For many years, we kept the peace. We patched up the tiny hole, as best we could, and they roamed free in our front and back gardens, among the gravel and weeds. One year, on a particularly hot summer, we delivered blue poison to their queen. Better their queen than our walls. I tried not to think about it. The next year, they came back, but kept mostly to themselves.

When we moved out of our house in the summer, we hired a professional gardener to clear out the wildness: the brambles and thistles; our out-of-control hedge. We did not ask our usual questions about methods. After they were done, our garden was transformed, neat and contained. The neighbour's landlord would be pleased. But that night, the ants descended upon us, through cracks we did not even know existed, crawling in multitudes all over our kitchen tiles. We had ruined their home.

Suppose that hungry ghosts transcend cultural and species boundaries. They come into being when their descendants neglect them, or after violent deaths. If you go far back enough, almost all our ancestors are hungry ghosts.

It takes surprisingly few generations to find a common ancestor for all of humanity. Scientists estimate that our most recent shared ancestor lived as recently as 1200 CE.[4] With each generation back, our number of ancestors grows exponentially, so even a few hundred years ago, we each have hundreds of thousands of ancestors. Around thirty-three generations back, or between 800 and 1,000 years ago, every person has more than 8 billion ancestors, around the population of the Earth today. This may seem counter-intuitive, but many are not 'unique' ancestors; they occupy more than one ancestral role due to species inbreeding.[5]

Hungry ghosts may be vengeful and eternally damned, as Chinese folk beliefs suggest. Somehow, this makes little sense to me. Their sorrow and rage, their ravening spirits, surely must carry some instruction, if not the possibility of redemption.

Part of me knew what the ghosts wanted all along, what they still want. It is not vengeance. Undoubtedly, their neglect in both life and death reveals that there are consequences for careless actions, however small or unintentional, which ripple through time and place. The obliteration of homes and species.

No, they want something else, but we refuse to listen. To tune in and tune out is not enough. They want us to face up to our broken obligations.

18. Ghosts of Chinatown

The smoke was too dark and thick to be a cloud. It hovered over the last standing building in Cranbrook's Chinatown as the sun set and the summer heat lifted from the pavement. We were the only ones on the street, visiting my grandfather's hometown during the record-breaking 2023 wildfire season in Canada. Most of the buildings were closed or boarded up, apart from an old brick inn with a neon 'open' sign and another advertising exotic dancers.

I wanted to walk the former streets of the Chinatown of my grandfather's youth before their memory disappeared completely. We were following a map that my grandfather sketched of Chinatown as he remembered it in the 1920s.

'This is it,' I said to my son, checking the address. 'This building is all that is left of Chinatown.'

'Mum,' he sighed as I stopped to take some photos. 'You've got to stay in the present moment.'

'But I am,' I protested. 'This is what we are here for, to see where your great-grandfather was born.'

'That's the past, not the present,' he said.

There was nothing obvious about the building to indicate that it had once been a part of Chinatown.

No faded lettering, no ornamental features, no commemorative plaque. I compared it with the grainy newspaper photo of the former Chinese Masonic Hall, built in 1952 after a fire razed the original. It was the same modest two-storey building, with a recessed balcony and painted wood panelling, now owned by a local Canadian business specializing in custom embroidery. On each floor, there was a central door flanked by two windows. Searching the hall for traces of its past, I noticed that it bore a faint resemblance to the Mah village clan hall, not the content but the form.

The original Chinese Masonic Hall in Cranbrook was constructed in 1921, a conversion of a disused two-storey building on Seventh Avenue, two doors away from my great-grandfather's store. It was an important meeting place for Chinese people in my grandfather's youth, back when the city's restaurants displayed 'white only' signs.

Cranbrook's Chinatown began as a small, segregated community of Chinese railroad labourers and Gold Rush miners in the late 1800s who lived across from the railway station. It expanded to include other Chinese migrants and their families, until the Chinese Exclusion Act of 1923, the law passed by the Canadian government prohibiting Chinese immigration, which was only repealed in 1947. By then, my grandfather and his brother and sister had left the city, unmoored after their father's sudden death on a solo trip back to China in 1935. Despite the racism my grandfather faced growing up – racist taunts, exclusion from white social events and 'alien immigrant' status despite being born in Canada – he wrote with affection about the lively frontier Chinatown nestled in the Rocky Mountains.

Now Chinatown was nearly erased from the city's memory, apart from sketchy recollections in local history books of a crowded jumble of gambling houses, shacks, laundries, stores, restaurants, gin joints and opium dens, all tightly packed on a few streets on the edge of the city between the red-light district and the Canadian Pacific Railway station.

My son tugged on my sleeve, anxious to get back to our hotel. Firefighting planes were flying low overhead towards the smouldering hills beyond the town. The sky seemed to belong to another planet, soft blue invaded by a cacophonous grey.

We walked back downtown, which looked disconcertingly like my childhood hometown, with its old-fashioned main street and alpine theme. Even the people, the stares I felt past and through me, the pick-up trucks revving their engines and blaring bass music, reminded me of the place I had left behind.

Our hotel was located on the main street, a boutique red-brick hotel renovated to restore some of its original 1920s feel, complete with Art Deco-style furniture and old newspaper clippings. In our room, a poster of a German warplane from the First World War hung over the television, which seemed like an unusual choice. It felt abrasive, somehow.

As my son flopped onto the bed, I checked the air quality levels. The current level was still 'low risk', but it was predicted to rise to 'moderate risk' by the morning and climb higher the next day. The wildfire had nearly tripled in size over the past twenty-four hours, several homes had been lost, and nearly a hundred people from the nearby ʔaq̓am Indigenous community had been evacuated.

I should have gone with my instincts. My first thought, after hearing the pilot's announcement earlier that day, was that we should get off the plane. Why fly into the middle of a wildfire? Not only might it be unsafe or difficult to get back out, but it seemed decadent. My son was scared. But the other passengers remained seated, seemingly unfazed. The women sitting across the aisle commented on how they had not been able to fly the day before and hoped this one would land. The cabin door locked, and the flight attendants began their safety demonstration.

The small city of Cranbrook is located on the Traditional Territory of the Ktunaxa Nation in the Kootenay valley region of southeast British Columbia. As the 'gateway to the Canadian Rockies', it is surprisingly difficult to get to, which also makes it difficult to get out of. Despite its incorporation in 1905 as a Canadian Pacific Railway (CPR) hub city, it no longer has a train station. The former CPR station is now a museum, where visitors are offered guided tours of defunct antique trains and invited to imagine the old Gold Rush passenger routes. The Greyhound buses in and out of the city stopped running years ago.

The ten-hour drive east to Cranbrook from Vancouver cuts through mountains, winds along cliff edges and requires sturdy brakes for the long and steep descents. I couldn't overcome my fear of driving, so I had booked the extra flight and suppressed the guilt. It was a real thing, the guilt. After three years of not flying due to Covid-19, the flight from London to Vancouver felt reckless, like ripping a hole through the Earth. And the flight to wildfire-encircled Cranbrook felt like another kind of recklessness altogether.

Yes, it was an oversight not to have checked the news before going to the airport. I only checked the weather, which looked sunny and warm, and the flight status, which said nothing about interruptions. Since arriving in Vancouver, we'd spent our time exploring the city, visiting Chinatown and the classical Chinese gardens, having lunch in the revolving restaurant at the Harbour Centre, and going to Science World. I was taking my therapist's advice: relax; focus on the things you can control; don't catastrophize. And my own: limit exposure to the news.

My dad watches the news every day, and he warned me about visiting Chinatown in Vancouver. During the pandemic, it got really bad, he said, full of tents and makeshift shelters in the streets, very unsafe and unhygienic. Now, it was getting better, but we should still be careful.

I wondered if he was thinking about someone else when he told me this, a cousin who was living on these streets. There was a silence around the memory of this cousin, the gnawing feeling of knowing yet not knowing where they were.

When I was an art student in Vancouver in the late 1990s, I took the bus every day through Chinatown and the neighbouring Downtown Eastside, past Pigeon Park, known for drug-dealing, and along the streets full of homeless people. Whenever relatives came to the city, we would go to Chinatown for dim sum, and even then, the restaurants were past their prime.

I was determined go to Chinatown on this trip, though, to visit the Chinatown Storytelling Centre and the newly opened Chinese Canadian Museum. Apart from fragments, I never heard stories about Chinese Canadian history when I was growing up.

We stayed in a hostel just a few blocks away from Chinatown and walked there after breakfast. As we got closer, my son asked about the funny smell.

The gateway arch to Chinatown is guarded by imperial concrete lions. Just beyond the arch, there was a man lying against a wall, head slumped to the side, unconscious. People walked past him as if he was not there.

The streets were lined with bright red lampposts. Some of the buildings were freshly painted, while others were derelict and covered in graffiti. We wandered past waving lucky cats, toy pandas and a neon rooster sign for chop suey. While we stopped to admire a mural about the history of Chinatown, we nearly tripped over a person in a sleeping bag.

After a few minutes, we found the Chinatown Storytelling Centre, located in a beautifully renovated red-brick building. It was a gem-like museum, with a shop selling books and gifts related to Chinese Canadian culture. The posters and objects on display in the exhibition were elegantly curated, and they gave me a small sense of pride. They told stories about the 15,000 Chinese labourers who came to British Columbia to complete the gruelling task of building the Canadian Pacific Railway through the Canadian Rockies, hundreds of whom died in the harsh conditions; the 'For a White Canada!' slogans and violent anti-Asian rallies of 1907; and the fact that Canada Day, which is celebrated on 1 July, was known as 'Humiliation Day' by Chinese Canadians because 1 July 1923 was the day when the Chinese Exclusion Act was passed. But for all the focus on past injustices, the injustices of the present were remarkably absent. The last panel of the exhibition, 'Chinatown Then and Now', simply stated that today's Chinatown was 'in steady decline' and in need of 'revitalization'.

On our way out of Chinatown, we saw a man in the middle of the street, staring blankly, mouth open, taking tiny jittery steps backwards while cars waited to pass. I had never seen a person in such a state. There is a new kind of drug, I learned later, that makes people look and act like zombies. In fact, it's been around for a while, I just hadn't been watching the news. But what kind of world is this, I thought, where we are supposed to see but not see, know but not know, and just keep walking?

By day three in Cranbrook, the smoke had reached dangerously unhealthy levels. It permeated the walls of our hotel and reminded me of my first trip to Beijing in the autumn of 2015, which had felt like entering an ashtray. We put on our facemasks, left over from Covid, and checked out of the hotel.

We had done everything I had wanted to: walked the former streets of Chinatown; visited the local library and the CPR museum; and dined in the only Canadian Chinese restaurant we could find. We even met a barber who remembered a relative of my grandfather's. For the most part, my research confirmed what I already knew. The only surprise was how little else there was. Chinatown was only a footnote in the local history books, and the CPR museum failed to mention Chinese labourers at all.

While we waited outside the hotel for a taxi to the airport, a message pinged on my phone. Our flight to Vancouver that afternoon was cancelled.

I would like to say that I didn't panic, but some kinds of panic are less obvious than others, and mine was the kind that burned quietly. After cancelling the taxi, I paced through the haze along the main street, with my son trailing behind, full of questions that I could not answer. A policeman noticed how lost we looked and listened sympathetically. He advised renting a car. Next, we tried a café with a wifi connection, but it was patchy, and the smoke followed us inside. In the café, I heard a woman on her phone, exclaiming, 'The air stinks, it's gross, it's a blueish, brownish grey.'

After a while, we went back to the hotel and booked in for another night. My son watched TV as I searched for ways to get out of the city. The wildfire had swelled to 2,600 hectares, up from 850 hectares the night before. There were no rental cars available. Eventually, I booked another flight the next morning, hoping for a clearing in the smoke.

Overnight, the airport was placed on evacuation orders, ready to close on short notice. As we approached the airport in the early morning, scarcely visible through the smoke, the taxi driver told me to call him if we needed a lift back into town. He doubted that any flights would be getting out. The airport was open, but there was hardly anyone inside. Gradually, as our departure time drew closer, a handful of other passengers arrived.

We watched the smog on the runway, which seemed to grow thicker by the minute. The plane that we were supposed to leave on couldn't land. The airline gate agent told us all we should go home and check back later, but many of us lingered, unsure what to do. One person was on their way to a funeral, another was a pilot, stranded far away from home, and another was a mother with a son just a few years older than mine.

As I mulled over the options – call my dad again, go back to the hotel, wait to see if any other planes would leave that day – I heard a woman's voice call out, 'Does anyone want a drive to Calgary?' She had a van and could take seven people. Calgary is a four-to-five-hour-drive away from Cranbrook, in the opposite direction to Vancouver, but at least the flights would be running.

'Yes, please!' I said immediately, almost without thinking.

The seats in the van were taken within minutes, five women plus two children, each with frayed nerves, and deeply grateful. We drove in silence for miles and miles through the smoke and trees. At first, I thought it was fog, or perhaps smoke from another fire, but it was all from the same one. After an hour or so, we finally reached clean air. The driver of the van was a local, and she knew the best stops for gas and food. She took us on the scenic route through the Rockies, where we spotted another smoking wildfire on a distant mountain range.

'Would you like to climb one of these mountains?' I asked my son.

'Actually yes,' he said, marvelling at their size. 'Maybe not one of the burnt ones, though.'

Months later, my son maintained that we would still be stuck in Cranbrook had it not been for the van. Certainly, the trip was instructive. It taught me about the helplessness yet normality of living in and through the climate crisis, how people keep carrying on.

We reached my parents' house on Vancouver Island well after midnight, taking the last flight from Calgary to Nanaimo. I can't remember falling asleep, but in the early hours before dawn, I woke up in the middle of a scream, as if inhabited by another being.

At breakfast, I mentioned the scream to my dad. I had never had a night terror before.

'It must have been the ghosts,' he said.

'I don't believe in ghosts,' I said, looking at him suspiciously.

'That doesn't change whether or not they are there,' he said with a smile.

PART THREE

Burnt Offerings

19. Incalculable Debts

'What are you afraid of?' The ancestral tour guide looked baffled. Suddenly, I felt ridiculous. I could not possibly tell him about the ghosts.

It would be dangerous to return without money, Lily had warned me over our last coffee in Shenzhen. Yet a part of me wanted to return one day, to show that it was possible, that no bridges had really been burned.

'Your ancestors will be happy,' the guide assured me. It would be enough just to return. The villagers would not expect any financial contributions now, he said, especially not after the pandemic. To travel thousands of miles would be enough, to show that we remembered. That would make them happy.

I wanted to believe him. It was the bit about travelling, though, that rang false. To travel thousands of miles just for a few days, as if it was effortless to burn through so much money and fuel, and then show up, yet again, with nothing?

Ancestral roots tourism is a popular business in South China. There are over 50 million overseas Chinese around the world, an international community spanning multiple generations. Many people in the Chinese diaspora have made emotional journeys to discover their ancestral villages and give offerings at temples and tombs.

Maybe, if we could find the tombs, that would be a reason to return. I could sweep them and feel some form of peace.

But what difference would that make? Hungry ghosts stay ravenous and insatiable forever.

To fly in and fly out is not enough. If anything, it only reopens old wounds.

I thanked the guide for his time. It was silly to think of travelling, anyway, when we were still in the middle of moving.

On the living room wall, my mom keeps a framed black and white photograph of her mother's father, Grandpa Stewart, when he was about eight years old, with wide eyes, long blond curls and a kilt. He grew up on a farm in a village in Quebec and left school after grade two, around the time the photograph was taken in the 1910s. Next to Grandpa Stewart are other black and white family photographs: my mom at the age of four sitting with her sister on top of a horse; and faded primary school photos of my mom's parents, taken in Ottawa.

I asked my mom once why she only displays photos of her family when they were children. She laughed and said it must be because that was when they were still innocent.

Stewart is one of ten Scottish surnames with ancient clan histories advertised by the National Tourist Board of Scotland. Many tourism companies in Scotland offer packages for visitors to discover their clan histories and the places where their ancestors might have once travelled.

Along the Royal Mile in Edinburgh, tourist shops sell a wide range of clan crest badges, tartans and booklets.

For a long time, I have been drawn to Scotland as a place, but never to the clans. My ancestors migrated from Scotland so long ago that any connection with clan histories seems distant at best. My mom's hand-drawn family tree traces her roots in Scotland as far back as the 1700s. Recently, her brother researched this ancestry and was surprised to discover that Grandpa Stewart was probably more Irish than Scottish, at least by blood, descended from Scots Irish in Northern Ireland, who emigrated to Quebec in the mid-nineteenth century during the Irish Potato Famine.

That side of my family has no stories from their time of emigration, though, apart from faint ties to the 'royal Stewarts'. The only story I have heard about Grandpa Stewart is that he probably should have been put in prison.

I was never particularly drawn to the Mah clan, either, before my trip to the village. Bloodlines are too insular and exclusionary. I only wanted a glimpse, to map the China of stories and imagination onto some-place real.

Something changed, though, when I met Uncle Mah and the rest of the clan. It was the first time anyone said to me, directly and unequivocally, 'You owe.'

Well, come to think of it, my mom's dad once said this to me when I was a teenager, but I refused to accept it.

My mom says I should not write about her side of the

family; the stories are too lurid. I respect this, with just one exception: what I owe to her deceased parents, the other side of my ancestors. It would be negligent to forget them.

That time when I was a teenager, my grandpa cursed at me and said that I was ungrateful, that in his day, children were treated like eagle chicks, kicked out of the nest so they could learn to fly. I owed him my unquestioning obedience, and respect for his authority. He felt, like many older generations do about younger ones, that my parents let me get away with too much. That is the only time I can remember letting my anger flare, kicking a chair across the room. It was not the principle that I objected to. It was the hypocrisy, knowing, as I knew then and probably should not have, about how he had treated his own children.

My grandma asked me to forgive my grandpa, but the way she said it, so lightly and accommodatingly, made me forgive him even less.

More than twenty years later, when the Mah clan said, 'You owe,' I wanted to accept it this time, to be a grateful and gracious granddaughter. A nervous laugh, a caricature of greed, an assurance of future happy returns . . . regardless, we owed.

On the face of it, what we owed the clan was quite literal. We owed money, generations' worth. My grandfather Mah described how he and his father relied on extensive clan networks to support their overseas studies and travels.[1] I do not think that they ever managed to settle their clan debts, which were mostly forgotten in the upheavals of war and revolution. My grandfather's uncles and cousins discouraged him from going to university because his father had lost all his savings in a bank collapse in Hong Kong, and his stepmother Aunt Wong wanted him to return to China. But return was not really an option in those tumultuous times. My grandfather managed to go to university anyway, paying some of his way by working at his uncles' café, while his clan relatives sent back what money they could to Aunt Wong.

What got to me was not just the recognition of debt. It was the impossibility of ever repaying it.

When we left the Mah village, I was overcome with a sense of obligation. I had a sort of wild idea, briefly, of making some kind of contribution, not a house, but a modest financial donation to the village, or even a small monument in place of either a home or a tomb, to mark our history there. Yet I knew that this was really the duty of a son, as a male Gold Mountain sojourner, and not of a granddaughter.

I also knew that I was not even considered Chinese. Lily and Ying told me that mixed-race identity is a foreign concept in rural China. Either a person is Chinese, or they are not. My dad's parents were forbidden from marrying outside of the Chinese community out of respect for their cultural traditions. Otherwise, my grandmother would have married a white man she met in northern Ontario instead of my grandfather.

When family histories are painful and complicated, what, if anything, do we owe our ancestors? I like to

consider my obligations in a spirit of generosity, hon-
ouring all ancestral wisdom, but this breaks down with
intergenerational trauma. There are too many untold
stories of the women in my family, whose names are
forgotten with each generation, cleaved off through
patrilineal lines.

Do we owe our ancestors proud monuments; respect
for their suffering and achievements; or simply compassion and forgiveness? My mom has been to Glasgow
before, for my wedding, and visited some places in Scotland where our ancestors might once have travelled. She
has no religion, but she forgives all sinners their
trespasses.

I wonder what I would say to my descendant, a great-
grandchild, who lives 100 years in the future. It is difficult
to imagine, maybe because it brings sadness and discomfort to think of a time beyond my own life. It also seems
vain to think any wisdom I carry now might be useful in
100 years. The times then will have their own challenges,
further into the sixth mass extinction. Yet I would like to
be able to offer something, if only just a few thoughts
about how to live with the ghosts.

There is a bridge between divided worlds, a place
where all spirits can rest without sorrow. The wounds
will not fester, the plagues will not return. It exists on
the Earth in the present. I keep searching for this place,
which is neither inside nor outside of myself. When the
wind blows just right, I edge a bit closer.

20. A Buddhist Path

As we packed up boxes for our move to Scotland, I examined each item, remembering how it came into my life. My favourite was a small bronze statue of the Buddha, from the mantelpiece in the kitchen, one of the few personal items my husband kept from his childhood. The statue is about six inches tall, a slim version of the Buddha, sitting in the lotus position with his left hand on his lap, palm open, and the other hand touching the Earth.

It is not quite true that I have no religion. If pressed, I would say that I am a secular Buddhist. I believe in the possibility of transcendence.

When my grandfather's family returned to their ancestral home in China in 1925, they went to the altar in the central room to light incense sticks and pay respects to our ancestors for a safe journey back from Gold Mountain. Ancestral tablets hung in their home altar, while clan records and carvings were kept in the local Buddhist temple, following traditional religious customs. During his stay in the village, my grandfather recalled reciting Confucian lessons in the all-boys' village school and attending Buddhist wedding and funeral ceremonies.

But my interest in Buddhism did not come from my family. I discovered Buddhism in a more roundabout way, as a teenager searching for belonging. I was learning classical piano, and when I got to high school, I met teenagers from hippie and folk musician families who shared my enthusiasm for music. Their parents had come to northern BC in the 1960s and '70s, filled with counter-cultural dreams. I borrowed books from my new friends' houses, *Zen and the Art of Motorcycle Maintenance*, Herman Hesse's *Siddhartha* and the psychedelic writings of Alan Watts, which completely changed my worldview. They told stories of people with divided selves, who made profound spiritual journeys of self-realization.

I am still drawn to transcendental spirituality, but I am afraid of its power to loosen my grip on reality. At certain moments in my life, I have thought of myself as someone who can see into other people's souls. I know that this is probably an illusion.

The first time it happened was when I was sixteen, at a New Year's Eve house party in my hometown, where I went with a friend and some older teenagers who we barely knew. There was very little for young people to do in our town, especially in the winter, when the temperature was constantly twenty degrees below Celsius. Immediately, I regretted going. The whole house was shaking with aggressive rock music. I sat uncomfortably with my friend in the basement, away from the noise upstairs. Sitting across from us was a boy who we had never met, pale-cheeked, glassy-eyed, and sick from too much drink. As he retched, I felt like I could see his spirit, a bright gentle light emanating from his body.

Those days, I no longer packed church dresses into my overnight bags on sleepovers with friends, but every week, I went to another kind of gathering, which my parents disapproved of even more. It was called Wind Circle, a youth group led by a middle-aged woman who had studied homeopathy, lived in the forest for many years hunting deer, and considered herself to be a channel to the spirit world. We were a group of about fifteen teenagers, mostly the children of hippie folk musicians in our town.

I went to Wind Circle out of curiosity. There was something alluring about becoming a member of this select group, by invitation only. In fact, I did not trust the Wind Circle leader. I disliked having to share our feelings as we passed the smudge (burnt sacred herbs, a ceremony appropriated from Indigenous traditions) around the circle at the beginning of each session. The spiritual channel readings were also disturbing. The leader's voice, normally soft, became gruff as she spoke about the details of our past lives. She told one boy that he had been a murderer in a past life, which struck me as a highly irresponsible thing to say. Apparently, I had never taken the human form before; my mission in this life was to learn the nature of trust.

Some elements of Wind Circle must have filtered through, though. During my high school lunch breaks, I would often walk along the forest trail behind the school, stand next to a giant pine tree and imagine that I was merging into its bark. I still shudder to recall those embarrassing years, when I wore broccoli in my hair and long flowing dresses, convinced that I could see things that others could not.

The next time I felt this way was eighteen years later, on a ten-day silent Vipassana meditation retreat in Suffolk near the east coast of England. Vipassana, which means 'insight' or 'special seeing', is a form of meditation that originated in Theravada Buddhism, the oldest existing school of Buddhism, which aims for the complete liberation of mind and the realization of Enlightenment.[1] I went with my husband a few months after we got married. He went to the men's retreat, and I went to the women's one, held separately in different buildings.

My husband came to Buddhism through studying mathematics and physics. When we first met, while studying in London, he told me that there are deep connections between the physics of 'minds-observing-nature' and core Buddhist ideas such as non-self (Anattā). It was a revelation to find out that Buddhism can be detached from New Age beliefs about supernatural beings and past lives, as a philosophy rather than a religion. Buddhism, as we both appreciate it, is a way of living in the world: recognizing suffering and impermanence; and extending kindness and compassion to all beings.

The Vipassana retreat was effectively a monastic bootcamp, beginning meditation every day at four o'clock in the morning and continuing until five o'clock in the afternoon, taking breaks only for food and short walks. In many ways, the practice resembled other forms of meditation we had tried, starting with focusing on the breath, and then moving our attention to different parts of the body. The key difference was the intensity, and the lofty spiritual goals.

One of the most intriguing aspects of Vipassana is that many people report experiencing subtle, mystical-sounding all-body sensations. I started experiencing these sensations, tingling across my skin, by the fifth day. It felt like progress, a reward for so many hours of meditation, although we were told to observe any sensations, whether pleasing or painful, with equanimity.

Looking back, the Vipassana sensations no longer seem so mystical. I have experienced many similar sensations since, except they have come uninvited. Doctors call them psychosomatic manifestations of stress.

I learned early on that the best way to avoid suffering through the meditation was to surrender myself as completely as possible to the discipline and technique. Any laziness, indulgence in non-meditative thoughts or minor subversions, such as singing softly during walks, would only create more difficulty in withstanding the long hours of meditation. A word that kept coming to mind, especially in the beginning, was 'relentless'. There was no way of escaping.

In the evenings, we listened to old recordings of lectures from the guru, Goenka, a former lay teacher from Burma, born to an Indian family, who started teaching Vipassana in India in 1969, with the aim of making it accessible to large numbers of people. After decades of teaching, Goenka's brand of Vipassana now has over a hundred centres around the world, run by student-teachers. It is not without controversy. There have been several incidents of people leaving the retreats in states of extreme mental distress, raising questions about the risks of meditation.[2]

When I emerged at the end of the retreat, it was as if I was re-entering the world from a sensory deprivation tank. The sky, trees and clouds were hyper-real, the clarity of perception startling. I found it difficult to speak and cried at the slightest thing. In those fragile moments, I was reminded of the former selves that I had buried away: my teen Buddhist-New Age-experimentation days; and the years in art college that followed, when I moved to Vancouver, threw out my long dresses and pretended I was someone else. For the first time, instead of dismissing my former selves, I embraced them.

The only Buddhist temple I have visited outside of the UK is the Temple of the Six Banyan Trees (Liurong Temple) in Guangzhou, which dates to 537 CE. I went there five years after the Vipassana retreat, just before my trip to the Mah village. It was a short walk from my hotel in the old town. The temple grounds were tucked away from the bustle, featuring an ornate octagonal flower pagoda, giant Buddha statues and incense burners, along-side banyan trees and pots of flowers. Several people wandered around, offering incense and fruits to the Buddha. The spring air was warm and fragrant, and I enjoyed sitting in the sun for a few minutes of tranquillity.

At the time, I struggled to make sense of the ritualistic side of Buddhism, what compelled people to present physical offerings before statues of the Buddha. Now, I wonder whether it is really so easy to separate the secular from the sacred, as they do in secular Buddhism.

Since the Vipassana retreat, I have not been on another meditation retreat, and my meditation practice has flagged. There are practical constraints, like being a parent. There are also some nagging frustrations. One of the main problems with seeking paths to Enlightenment is that this possibility, while technically open to any human, has almost never been achieved. Even the Dalai Lama does not claim to have reached Enlightenment. Nor am I convinced that 'ego dissolution', one of the neurophysiological linkages between advanced meditative states and psychedelic drug use, is beneficial for mental wellbeing.[3]

Feeling the pain of trees that are sliced; communing with a world that is dying; tuning into the hungry ghosts: this was the next time in my life that I thought I could see into other beings' souls. It came without meditation, and without effort. At times, it felt like a form of evisceration.

As I faced the half-filled boxes in my office, I leafed through a book on Chinese Buddhism. An interesting story caught my attention, which I hadn't noticed before.

There is an ancient legend about a disciple of the Buddha who ventured into hell to rescue his mother from the realm of hungry ghosts. This disciple, named

Mu Lian in Chinese (Maudgalyayana in Buddhist texts), used his supernatural powers to try to feed his mother, but the food burst into flames as soon as it touched her lips. He was finally able to save his mother through the intervention of the Buddha, who advised him to prepare ritual food offerings to the community of monks on the fifteenth day of the seventh lunar month. Mu Lian followed these instructions and managed to liberate his mother and hundreds of other hungry ghosts from hell. This is the origin story of the Hungry Ghost festival.[4]

Contrary to Chinese folk religious beliefs about the need to pacify hungry ghosts, Mu Lian's tale highlights the possibility of salvation, which is achieved through a singular offering instead of one that needs to be perpetually repeated.

The hungry ghosts still clung to me, weighing me down while I prepared for our move, but I knew what I had to do. Search for an offering. Neither fruit nor incense would suffice, nor would a set ritual. It should be something uniquely my own, but also beyond myself, communal and facing outward. Something like the gifts of knowledge and teaching, normally offered by monks (*dharma*), but less clean and more imperfect, reflecting life on a contaminated planet. My skin tingled all over at the possibilities.

21. Dirty Oil Road

We inspected the toilet, which had never looked so sparkling, and then locked our front door for the last time. Despite the frequent rumble of passing trains, our house in Coventry had a calm energy about it, filled with light from the bay window overlooking the garden. I nodded a quiet thanks. I was working on 'gratitude', a type of meditation that is supposed to help with anxiety. Zen Buddhists like to thank the toilet after each use, an idea that makes me smile.[1]

A one-way journey is disorienting; the mind still thinks of the place left behind as home. Our old furniture and belongings felt clumsy in the new space. We heard strange night-time sounds – animal cries, creaks in the tenement below, voices in the walls. In the fuzzy days after arrival in Glasgow, it seemed as if we were wandering in an otherworldly realm. The summer air was warm and heavy with pollen; the streets brimmed with exuberance.

From the grassy lookout by the University of Glasgow's tower, we could see wind turbines in the surrounding hills. It is comforting to see the edges of a city, the suggestion of an escape route. By 2050, stretches of land along the banks of the River Clyde are projected to be below the annual flood level, while the higher ground of the city remains above it, unlike so many other riverine cities around the world.[2] But nobody can predict when the next disaster will strike, or what form it will take.

I made little rules for myself. I would live more in accordance with my values; limit long-distance travel; focus on recovery; spend more time with family; explore places close to our new home. It was a private bargain with the ghosts, to try to keep them away. Yet part of me knew they would follow me anyway.

The first place I wanted to visit was Grangemouth, the petrochemical town on the Firth of Forth, where I had done research just before the pandemic. It was a half-hour train journey east of Glasgow. The week of our move coincided with Climate Camp Scotland, an autonomous group campaigning against fossil fuels and for climate justice, which had chosen Grangemouth for their annual week of action. Grangemouth is a former BP (British Petroleum) oil boom town. Its sprawling refinery complex, fuelled by North Sea oil and fracked shale gas shipped from America, has been owned by the controversial petrochemical giant INEOS since 2005.

My introduction to Grangemouth's dramatic skyline, 'alight with tinsel and chimneys and spires', was in April 2019.[3] I had wanted to visit it for years, after observing it only from a distance. On family holidays in Scotland, my son loved playing with his cousins by the Kelpies, a pair of monumental steel horse heads standing 100 feet tall in a park built on derelict scrubland between the towns of Falkirk and Grangemouth.

I took the train to the nearest station, where I met Bryan, an environmental activist and local resident, who offered to take me on a walking tour of Bo'ness Road, the 'dirty oil road' that runs through the middle of the petrochemical complex and includes several of Scotland's top polluters.[4] Over the past ten years, Bryan had brought many people along this road, by bicycle or car rather than on foot, including diplomats, politicians, journalists and filmmakers. He saw the role of these tours as educational, to show people the 'connections that are all present along one road'. Sometimes, they were stopped by the police, so we had to be careful.

It is unusual for a public road to run directly through the heart of a petrochemical complex, and INEOS wanted to close it. But there was a great deal of local opposition to the planned closure, Bryan said, more so than environmental concerns. The road had been there for a long time, and people used it as the main road to access services and different areas.

As we approached the top of Bo'ness Road, we passed the former BP social club and sports grounds, where people were out playing football, with the petrochemical smokestacks looming beyond. Bryan recalled that people used to feel proud of their town and the benefits that the oil company brought, like the social club. He had felt safe growing up there because his dad worked at BP. Yet as he grew older, he became increasingly worried about the threat of nuclear war. The first group he joined was the Campaign for Nuclear Disarmament 'because in the eighties, like you'd be walking to school knowing you were the biggest target in Scotland because of the oil industry, and if they dropped one nuclear bomb it would be in Grangemouth'.[5]

Bryan was also concerned about climate change and acid rain, but his turning point towards environmental activism came when he left school at the age of seventeen during the Thatcher years, when oil companies were cutting workers' wages, rights and jobs. He could not get a job at the BP plant, like his dad had been able to. 'You weren't given that life-changing career option that everybody else had been given,' he said.

Gradually, local jobs in the industry declined, due to rising automation and the recruitment of high-skilled workers from outside of town.[6] In 2005, BP left, selling the company to INEOS, a private enterprise owned by billionaire Jim Ratcliffe. Bryan was bitter about the sale. He showed me a BP brochure that he had kept, the advert for the BP industrial site, which he compared to selling a house. INEOS revived the remaining industry through expansion into fossil fuel supply lines and dealt a crushing blow to the trade union during a strike in 2013.[7] Within a decade, it had become one of the top ten petrochemical companies in the world.

The walk along Bo'ness Road took about an hour, starting with the oil refinery at the top end, followed by power plants, storage tanks and petrochemical infrastructure. As we walked past the stark industrial landscape along the side of the busy traffic, Bryan told me that the industry was invisible to people because they had lived next to it all their lives. He repeated this observation a few times, which was striking, given how close and unavoidable it was.

Towards the end of the dirty oil road tour, near the hotel where I was staying, Bryan pointed out a pesticide plant and said that this was the most toxic part of the industry, how oil gets into food. Maybe it was the power of suggestion, but just then, it hit me, that noxious petrochemical smell.

Bryan could smell it too. He told me a story about working in the mail room in the industrial area one summer and getting taken out with the mail van: 'The guy was saying, "Can you smell that?" and I was like, "Yeah," and it was like, "Well, if you can smell it you're okay, but when it gets to a higher concentration you can't smell it, and that's when you're at risk".'

I went to Grangemouth again in October 2019 with my research team to conduct focus groups and interviews with residents about their experiences of living in a petrochemical town. This turned out to be my last research trip before the pandemic. We held focus groups in a reception room in a local hotel, and there was a good turnout, around twenty participants. The main theme that came out of the discussions was frustration at the decline and neglect of the town over decades, and at the disconnection between the deprivation in local communities and the obscene wealth of INEOS.[8]

The personal account that stayed with me the longest was from a man in his early sixties, whose back garden faced directly over the plant. Like Brytan, he had tried to get a job in BP when he was young but was unable to get in, so he had found other work. He hesitated before sharing his complaints, saying that they were 'a bit selfish', as if he was worried about betraying his town. But then he described the dust in his back garden, sleepless nights because of the 'unbearable noise', and how his wife 'absolutely hates the place'. [9] The incessant pollution brought continuous stress to him and his family.

'I tell you it's that bad,' the man said. 'If the flares are going up, we turn our lights off in the house, and we can all see what's going on. It lights the garden, and this year has been a pretty terrible year because you just can't separate it. There's no peace.'

I have often felt uncomfortable about doing research in areas of decline and pollution. I wrote about this discomfort ten years ago, in an essay on the 'dereliction tourist'.[10] One of the most difficult things I faced in my research in different communities living with industrial ruination was the expectations from residents of what I could offer them. Many people seemed to think that through telling me their stories, they could secure better housing, working and living conditions, and less polluted air.

It occurs to me that I was haunted then by the same issue as I was in the Mah village: the weight of unfulfilled expectations. I don't know why I kept circling back.

Yet there was something I did not think about when I wrote that essay: the healing power of storytelling. Bryan told me that he wanted to share people's stories, and that he learned through studying community education that telling stories can be an effective way to make change.

He contrasted Grangemouth with other polluted petro-chemical communities in South Africa and North America that he had learned about, where there were 'bucket brigades' to monitor air pollution. He said that Grangemouth, while being the most polluted area in Scotland, was also heavily monitored, and that they didn't need more monitors. One of his personal projects was to collect stories of residents about when they first noticed that they lived next to an oil refinery. He wanted to draw people's attention to the 'invisible' threat that they all faced.

Kinneil Estate and Nature Reserve in the town of Bo'ness seemed an odd choice for Climate Camp, since it was a half-hour bus journey from Grangemouth, but it was close to the dirty oil road. Through a small gap in the stone garden wall beside the old Kinneil mansion, my son and I found the entrance to the camp. The path opened onto a large grassy field, bordered by thick oak and lime trees, giving it a feeling of safety. There were fewer people than I had expected, and the mood was subdued, like the groggy Sunday morning of a summer music festival. There were several large white tents set up for speeches and activities, people making coffee and queuing for the organic toilet, and a hodgepodge of small tents assembled in the grass.

The organizers had asked me to contribute to a community outreach hub in Grangemouth that afternoon, including scientists and medics who were concerned about the climate crisis, and I wanted to touch base with the camp first.

My son and I walked tentatively among the large tents, stopping for a few minutes to read the programme of activities for the day, and receiving warm welcomes from camp volunteers.

One of the camp coordinators, an older woman who was dashing about the site, came up and asked if I was one of the people going to the community hub. I said yes, and she beamed and said she was relieved because numbers were low. She introduced me to some climate activists from different parts of Scotland who had been assigned to the hub. One young activist came from Aberdeen, the 'oil capital of Europe'. He complained that he could not find anyone in that city to talk to about the climate crisis. I could feel his anxiety, eclipsing my own.

I was pleased to meet some new friends but disappointed that there were so few local people. The town of Grangemouth, including all the toxic polluting industries along Bo'ness Road, is in an area with a high risk of flooding from three local rivers and the Firth of Forth estuary. This risk is projected to increase over the next few decades, threatening many homes, businesses and industries.[11] Already, Grangemouth was a priority area for hundreds of millions of pounds' worth of funding for flood protection from the Scottish government and Falkirk Council, due to the risks posed to 'national infrastructure'.[12] Another 'invisible' threat.

While the camp broke for lunch, my son and I sat on a wooden bench surrounded by a semi-circular wall of interweaving stones and put on our raincoats. There was a faint mist of rain and dark grey clouds gathering over the trees.

A young man with a beard and tousled hair, and socks pulled over his trousers, sat down beside us and pulled an old-fashioned typewriter out of his bag. He put it on his lap and asked if we would like to write a story with him.[13]

'How much does it cost?' I asked, a little wary, and he smiled and said it was free; he wrote stories for strangers. My son was up for it.

They sat together and discussed ideas for storylines, and the words began to flow. The title was 'Black Holes', my son's favourite topic, about the end of the Earth, stretched apart and swallowed by two black holes, and the birth of a tiny new world.

22. Foraging

In the city, there is an illusion of abundance: cafés, super-markets and restaurants all around. Yet as crops fail and global supply lines falter, people will need to relearn ways of living off the land. Most cities are vulnerable to ecological threats, lacking in self-sufficiency, reliant on dense infrastructures of commerce and industry.

One of the most famous theories of the city is the concentric circle, developed by American sociologist Ernest Burgess in 1925, which described urban growth emanating from the central business district to the suburban fringes, along class lines.[1] I learned about this outdated theory as a student in London twenty years ago, part of a group of budding sociologists researching cities. We also studied the destructive side of urban growth, how it eats up the productivity of workers and land. Destruction was my area of specialism.

Now, I was back in a department of urban social scientists in Glasgow, moving into the bustling West End. The irony was that I still knew little about city life, carrying my small-town origins wherever I went, too trusting of strangers, skittish around crowds.

When I moved to Vancouver after high school, I found myself in all kinds of awkward conversations on the bus, and it took a while before I learned to avoid eye contact. A few years later, in Montreal, I knew better, and stayed in the library most of the time. London, though, was the city that overwhelmed me. It was a stretch to live there, even with a scholarship, and lonelier than I had expected. I rented a tiny, cold room above a Chinese restaurant in the East End, beside a railway line and a pub with a barking dog chained outside. I suffered from insomnia throughout the first winter. On the week-ends, I paced, walking back and forth through streets and parks, and along the river, slowly widening my circle.

I like the idea of concentric circles in the city, not as a model for how it functions, but as a metaphor for a mode of exploration, inching and spiralling outwards, away from a given point of arrival. The notion of gradually increasing circles suggests possibilities, on a collective level, of openness and interconnection. But in practice, there are many barriers to crossing such boundaries.

During our first months in Glasgow, I felt no urge to move beyond a limited sphere. Fatigue hit me, unfamil-iar after years of hyper-alertness. My body resisted it intensely, my stomach lurching, but I could not over-come the exhaustion. Maybe it was just an extension of the jetlag after our trip to BC, but it followed a pattern, pervading the summer lull of holidays and heat.

On Vancouver Island, we spent hours filling baskets full of wild blackberries, which grow in bushes next to the sidewalks and beaches. My sister-in-law showed my son how to make jam. When we got back to Glasgow, he added 'berry-picker' to his growing list of future jobs.

We were grateful for the shared gardens outside of

our rented flat, which were frequented by a grey-brown fox. From our third-floor tenement window, we could see the fox sniffing around the gardens in circles, following the same path every evening at dusk.

My great-grandfather Mah arrived in Nanaimo on Vancouver Island in 1898, planning to join his clan relatives in mining for coal, or 'Black Gold', but he discovered that the government had passed a law prohibiting the Chinese from underground mining. Instead of facing the heavy labour of the laundry, which was the other main work available, he set out to try his luck in the goldfields. His clan relatives thought that it was a lucky omen that the gold claims were at Wild Horse Creek, 'befitting them of the MAH-horse clan'. My great-grandfather joined another Taishanese labourer for the 400-mile journey through rugged mountain country along the Dewdney packhorse trail. As young, adventurous Taishanese people, they were 'not afraid of mountains', and walked in with miner mules carrying their goods and supplies.[2]

Yet with few habitations along the trail, they might not have survived the journey, had it not been for the kindness of strangers. While the white miners were unfriendly towards them, local scouts were sympathetic and taught them how to fish with a hook and line. Indigenous people showed them edible berries, roots and vegetation, including wild spinach, which my great-grandfather called 'horse manure greens' because it sprouted around the horse droppings.

At Wild Horse Creek, my great-grandfather joined other Chinese sojourners in reworking abandoned gold claims before taking a job as a bookkeeper and store-keeper for a railroad contractor. When the railroad was completed, he moved to the new town of Cranbrook, a few miles northeast of Wild Horse Creek, to set up his business with clan relatives in Chinatown.

My great-grandfather's rented family bungalow was located on the edge of the town. Just beyond it, there was a 'mecca' of wild berry bushes, with saskatoons, strawberries, raspberries, blueberries, wild cherries, gooseberries, loganberries and rose hips. My grand-father described his delight at playing among the bushes, flowers and insects as a child, and pride at how well his mother adapted to life in Cranbrook during the early years, planting a Chinese vegetable garden in their back-yard and converting the stable into a chicken coop.[3]

Despite experiencing racist taunts when he was growing up in Cranbrook, my grandfather recalled many acts of kindness and generosity from people outside the Chinese community. Children from white railway workers' families accompanied my grandfather and his siblings during their walks to and from school, offering them protection from bullies.

There was also solidarity between Chinese and Ktu-naxa people in Cranbrook. The Ktunaxa people often sold firewood to my grandfather's clan relatives for their stoves, and brought them fish and game, which they could give but not sell, according to tribal rules. One time, their closest Ktunaxa friend brought them a porcupine, which came as a surprise. With a touch of humour, my grand-father recalled that 'Cousin Jack used the steamed cat recipe with wine and herbs which turned out well, so we called it "pinetree cat" (Tone Shee Meow).'[4]

Maybe I took it for granted, but I did not like the tedium of gardening as a child, the constant watering and weed-ing, the itchy eyes. My mom kept an extensive flower bed that curved along the side of our lawn, full of per-ennial flowers that would bloom from spring through autumn. We planted a vegetable garden every spring, with chives, snow peas, carrots, green beans, chard and potatoes. In the back garden, there was an overgrown tangle of raspberries and strawberries, and two huge patches of rhubarb. Our dog used to slurp the raspber-ries straight from the bushes. In the front garden, beside a stand of birch trees, was a lone blueberry bush, where we had buried our dead cat. I never wanted to eat those blueberries.

I preferred mountain pine, cedar and juniper trees, and devil's club, which was a traditional medicine that could be used to make tea and connect to the spirit world.

Coventry was the first place I ever tried keeping a garden as an adult. I did not think I would miss its wildness.

From our front window in Glasgow, our son looked out at the shared gardens longingly, asking when we could plant our own vegetables again, and if we could plant berry bushes.

One Sunday towards the end of summer, I booked us

onto a foraging walk at a nearby country park, hoping it would help us to get our bearings. The guide was a self-taught foraging enthusiast, who had recently survived for a month through foraging alone, supplemented by wild deer, which had been shot during culls. There were only two other participants, hikers who wanted to learn about the foods that they could eat in nature. The walk began magically enough, learning about the energy bursts you can get from female nettle seeds; how to identify the softest, most delicate lime leaves; and thin dark leaves that smell of vanilla. I had not come prepared for what is perhaps the most obvious aspect of foraging: the identification not only of foods, but of poisons.

There are many false friends in the world of foraging, especially in the carrot family. Some are sweet and delicious, while others are deadly. The guide showed us a patch of cow parsnip, which resembles poison hemlock, and how to tell the two apart. She offered us a bite. My husband and I tried it, somewhat reluctantly, but our son refused. The leaves tasted bland and bitter. I wondered: was it worth the risk? Under what situation would we really need to eat cow parsnip?

The mushrooms were also disconcerting. We found one edible variety, and another poisonous, which led the guide to talk about an unusual case of mushroom poisoning in the news, before stopping partway through when she remembered our son's age.

Our guide seemed to take a strange relish in identifying the most poisonous plants, even more so than the edible ones. She was particularly pleased to find a yew tree and told us how just a few of its red berries could kill an adult human. Then, she asked us if we would like to taste the sweet red flesh of the berry, the outer part surrounding the poisonous seeds, because apparently this was okay to eat in tiny amounts. One of the hikers wanted to try it, for 'the thrill', but the rest of us declined. I learned later that the yew tree is commonly found in church graveyards, to keep devils and animals away, and it is a symbol of death and rebirth in ancient Celtic beliefs. Still, I keep a wide berth whenever I see one now.

By foraging, I wanted to escape poisons, which I associated with the synthetic world, but of course, they are everywhere, part of the natural world too. Towards the end of the walk, as we came to a small river, the guide turned to the other kind of poisons: how plants that used to grow along the river no longer did so, and how the water was no longer safe to swim in.

If the water was not safe to swim in, I asked, what about the plants on its shores, the wild strawberries and young plantain leaves that we had picked? We could wash them if we were worried about it, the guide advised.

In the days that followed, my son noticed female nettle seeds, lime leaves and plantain leaves along the side of streets in Glasgow's West End. I would not let him pick them. We were in the city, I said, and who knew what chemicals had been sprayed, or what dogs had urinated on the plants. Toxic contamination was my own form of knowledge, I realized, and could be helpful to pass on to future generations.

*

Things that seem innocuous can hurt you, sometimes quickly, but often slowly, delaying their deadliness for years or even decades into the future. Swimming. Antibiotic- and chemical-contaminated sewage in rivers, lakes and oceans, seeping into your skin and blood. Breathing. Exposure to fine particulate matter, nitrogen dioxide, asbestos fibres, things that get into your lungs. Sleeping. Volatile organic compounds from off-gassing carpets, paints and furniture, irritating your eyes, nose and throat. Praying. Toxic pollutants from burning candles and incense, contaminating sacred spaces.

Yet fear is also toxic, increasing our vulnerability to illnesses. We need guides to identify poisons, so we can learn to live more calmly and vigilantly among them, and find ways of healing.

23. Sound

The wounds and sorrows of the Earth are heavy. Some-times, you just need to sit with them. To see and to know, this is the first step. But if you lean in too much, you risk being spaghettified, sucked into a black hole. Nothing can come back out of a black hole in its original form.

In the *Tipitaka* (Triple Canon), the Buddha spoke of blessings for those seeking happiness: vast learning in handicraft; supporting family; peaceful livelihoods; rev-erence, humility and gratitude; and other blessings of the Holy Life. Only one besides Enlightenment seems unattainable: 'If a man's mind is sorrowless, stainless, and secure, and does not shake when touched by the worldly vicissitudes – this is the Highest Blessing.'[1] How can the mind not shake?

My mind shook more, not less, in the first months in Glasgow. It was the sound. Low rumbles, shouts, engines, footsteps. Glasgow has a population of over 620,000 people, around twice the size of Coventry, but it felt much bigger, and louder.

There was a constant drumbeat, rhythmic, incessant, thumping across the city. We thought it might be a marching band, practising, but the beats were far too regular. They started early in the morning and continued into the evening. Eventually, we discovered what the sound was because some residents filed noise complaints. It was happening down on the Clyde: industrial piling, driving foundations deep into the ground to build new warships. They had planning permission.

'You have not yet been through a winter,' my new colleagues told me knowingly, as if it was a rite of passage to weather a Glasgow winter before claiming to belong there. But already, I knew that there was something melancholic about the city, which exceeded the seasons. This is part of what drew me in.

The first time I visited Glasgow was in the summer of 2005, after a year of living in London. I was writing my thesis on deindustrialization and intrigued by the city's history of shipbuilding. From my arrival at the train station, I walked west along the Clyde, which was more down-at-heel than I had expected, even in the daylight, and then north to my hostel, where guests were smoking marijuana in the lounge.

At the top of my list of places to visit was the Necropolis, a Victorian cemetery on top of a hill just east of the city centre, the burial grounds of Glasgow's merchant elites: sugar and tobacco barons; shipbuilders; plantation owners; and the odd poet. As I walked along the road leading up to it, I came across a parade of people marching to drums and carrying large flags. A thin, older man came up beside me and began speaking to me in a strong Glaswegian accent, telling me how he felt about the Orange marchers. He said that they were horrible people, celebrating the murders of Catholics, but I could not make out much else. He followed me up the hill as the marchers passed, continuing to vent his anger. I finally lost him when I got to the entrance to Glasgow Cathedral. It was the Church of Scotland, and he would not set foot in it.

The cathedral felt cold and unwelcoming, its grey sandstone walls covered in lavish memorials to army officers who had died during nineteenth-century colonial wars in India, China, Egypt and Afghanistan. Normally, I liked cemeteries, but the decaying opulence of the Necropolis beyond it seemed unusually grim.

Now, nearly two decades later, I thought of Glasgow as a place of return, where my husband and I had visited every summer and Christmas for years, walking from Glasgow Central to his granddad's flat in Garnethill, near the Glasgow School of Art. His granddad would serve us tea and biscuits, tell us stories about his travels during the Second World War, and show us his 'rogues gallery' of family photographs.

We walked past old book and record shops by the River Kelvin, which my husband used to visit with his dad, and their former flat in Maryhill, a working-class area in northwest Glasgow. A concrete sculpture of an elephant still stood on their street, looking rather forlorn.

But maps of the past do not quite match the present. And the world continues to fall apart. Genocidal war; destructive floods and cyclones; the hottest year since records began. Some neuroscientists say that we have 'mirror neurons', reflecting the pain and distress of other living organisms we interact with, so 'it is no surprise that when the world breaks, we break with it'.[2]

The days stretched and folded, changing shape with the clouds. I made new friends in the climate movement who were committed to non-violent direct action – Quakers, Christians, doctors. We discussed climate despair over homemade soup and bread.

Since the ghosts began to take hold of me, there was something that I could not understand: why I cried when I heard hopeful stories, more often than raw stories of loss. Especially ones about imagined bright green futures, where ancestral wisdom is honoured, and violence and poverty disappear, centuries of damage reversed. I did not want to admit that, maybe, it was because hope was the thing I had lost.

'Is it true that it rains all the time in Glasgow?' a professor asked me over a Zoom call from Spain. We were discussing some ideas for a conference talk about toxic pollution.

'Yes,' I said. 'Well, most of the time.' I tried to make a joke about it, but suddenly he grew serious.

'It really is a problem here,' he sighed. It hadn't rained for many months in the region where he lived in south-east Spain. He was perhaps a decade older than me and came from a family of olive grove farmers, passed on for many generations. For the past few years, their olives had failed to grow.

'It is very sad,' he said. 'The way of life of my family, and the people in my region, will be lost.'

He spoke with such despondency that I did not know what to say, except that I was sorry.

Until this conversation, I had never thought about what I might lose in the climate crisis, not specifically anyway, beyond unnamed disasters, enveloping whole cities and landscapes. Nor what I had already lost. It always seemed too small, too privileged, to think about it on a personal level, when so many people were suffering and dying on the frontlines.

In the climate crisis, people experience loss. It is palpable, in the here and now, in struggles over lives, lands and livelihoods. It is visceral, evoking grief over past and present losses, magnified into fears for the future.

I feared the loss of safe places. Of clean air, water and land. Of abundance and fertility.

I feared the loss of oboe reeds, made of the grass plant *Arundo donax*, giant reeds that grow in wetlands and riverbanks around the world, also used for clarinets and bassoons. They are an invasive species in most places, widely contaminated from harmful chemical substances, and highly flammable, increasing the risk of wildfires.[3] Within threatened ecosystems, reeds for wind instruments may not have high priority on the list of things to save. Yet nothing else can produce the sweet, sorrowful sound of the oboe, the closest sound of any instrument to the human voice.

The wooden door to the music teaching room at the end of the corridor swung open, and a man with warm, smiling eyes stepped out and greeted us enthusiastically, extending his arms to invite us inside. He was excited to have a new young oboist to teach.

In this small room at the Royal Conservatoire of Scotland, I witnessed, for the first time in my life, teaching as a gift of pure joy. My son's teacher had a way of bathing a person in his full attention, making jokes that delighted and surprised, exuding love for their 'weird and wonderful instrument'. It felt like being in a divine presence. My son was completely enthralled.

Unpacking my books in my office, I prepared to welcome my own new students. I glanced through the depressing titles, variations of toxicity, pollution, injustice and catastrophe, and was struck by a sinking realization: I had devoted much of my life to the wrong questions. It was better to put joy out into the world, surely, than to add to the heaps of despair.

24. Light

There are inner poisons, as well as outer poisons. Seeping out, contaminating everything around them, like oil spills. Greed, guilt, shame. They are not just the cravings of hungry ghosts. They go much deeper, to the source of the injury.

When you are told that your ancestors were morally and spiritually corrupted, it leaves a psychic mark. A relentless drive to find and scrub out all poisons of the soul. I have been doing this for as long as I can remember, scrutinizing the jokes and rumours in my family, which run on both sides, mirroring each other: we are sinners, heathens, barbarians. Yet through searching for troubles, you call them into being, and they perpetuate.

It is difficult to eradicate the poisons of the soul if you do not believe in the soul's existence. In Buddhism, belief in a separate, permanent soul (or self, if a soul corresponds to a self) is an illusion, the cause of our suffering, alienating us from our interconnectedness with the universe. Materialist views of science also negate the concept of a soul, but for the opposite reason, imagining that we are all just complex mechanistic configurations of atoms and neurons.[1]

There is no equivalent to the Christian idea of an indivisible soul, either, in Chinese folk religious beliefs.

The closest idea to the soul or spirit (*ling-hun*) is divided into several parts, most commonly two or three, but sometimes as many as ten or twelve. The dual notion of the soul comes from Taoism, split into *hun* (heavenly, godly, active, spiritual and male) and *p'o* (earthly, ghostly, receptive, bodily and female), reflecting cosmic dualisms of *yang* (*hun*) and *yin* (*p'o*). The three-way division of the soul corresponds to the places where the soul goes after death in Confucian traditions of ancestor worship, with different parts inhabiting the grave, ancestral tablet and underworld, each requiring different rituals of care.[2]

A divided soul, an illusory self, elusive poisons. But some things should not be reflected on, according to the Buddha, because they cause defilements in the mind to arise. Things like the existence or non-existence of the self. Apparently, it is unwise to ask questions such as: 'Did I exist in the past? Did I not exist in the past? What was I in the past? . . . Shall I exist in the future? What shall I be in the future?' This is called 'becoming enmeshed in views; a jungle of views, a wilderness of views'.[3]

Nor should we reflect too much on poisons. The Buddha identified three poisons of the mind: lust, hatred and delusion. We need to recognize and destroy these negative mental attitudes, he said, but we should not dwell on them. Poisons cause sickness. Only through cultivating positive attitudes of the mind – generosity, loving kindness and wisdom – can we dispel its poisons.

Lightness can break through darkness, very slowly, but it is not a linear process. It helps, in a city where it rains so much that the pavements slide under your shoes, where the bins spill over with empty drinks cans, and you don't expect the days to be sunny, but there is still plenty of kindness in the streets.

On High Street, the oldest street in Glasgow, down the hill from the cathedral, there is a mural of St Mungo, the patron saint of Glasgow, wearing a woolly hat and a hoodie, performing a miracle of bringing a dead robin back to life. His face is gentle and luminous, so vividly lifelike that he could be a portrait of someone you know, or wish you knew. St Mungo was a sixth-century missionary who set up a church where Glasgow Cathedral now stands, and his bones lie buried beneath its floor. I missed the sign marking St Mungo's holy remains on my first visit.

With each step towards lightness, there is a change in perspective. Small things, noticing birdsong, marvelling at how clouds form, rain falls and sun breaks through in a single morning. An intangible sense of interconnection.

25. Shipyards

The only tangible, material connection between my great-grandmother Woo and Glasgow is the ship that she and her daughter sailed on from Hong Kong to Vancouver in May 1914, the *Empress of Russia*. It was built at Glasgow's Fairfield shipyard in Govan on the south of the River Clyde, launched in 1912 and completed in 1913, one of a series of *Empress* ocean liners commissioned for the Canadian Pacific Steamship Company. Back then, Glasgow was at the height of its shipbuilding prowess, making some of the largest merchant and navy ships in the world, powered by steam from coal.

I know which ship my great-grandmother and her daughter arrived on because this information is recorded in a logbook in the General Registers of Chinese Immigration to Canada, a list of Chinese immigrants who arrived in Canadian ports between 1885 and 1949, created in Ottawa, and microfilmed in the National Archives of Canada. Names: Woo Shee (Mrs Mah Su); Mah Toy Yell. Occupations: merchant's wife; merchant's daughter. Ages: 35; 8. Remarks: Cranbrook, BC. Facial marks or peculiarities: small scar outer ear, small pit right cheekbone, small mole right forehead (Woo Shee); scar centre left cheek, small light pit front left ear, small pit above left eyebrow (Mah Toy Yell).[1]

The ship that brought my great-grandmother and her family back to Hong Kong in 1925 was the SS *Tyndarius*, a transatlantic liner built during the First World War further west along the Clyde, registered at the port of Liverpool. Each Chinese immigrant who sailed on the *Tyndarius* in 1925 has their own page in the General Register, including a photograph. The solemn young faces of my grandfather Henry at seven, my great-uncle Bill at six and my great-aunt Alice at nine peer out from 23 April 1925, giving official notice of their 'desire to leave Canada with the intention to return', approved by the Chinese Immigration Branch of the Department of Immigration and Colonization.[2]

I like ships, although I know that they are heavy polluters. Ships are connected to my roots, like the railroads in Canada, carrying migrants, made through backbreaking labour. The industrial veins of a shapeshifting global era, with double-edged legacies. So specific, a single ship, named, a floating place, traversing cultures.

I have never travelled on a ship before, only on ferries. The closest I got was a glimpse of a small cargo ship at the port of Marseille, in 2013, when I was doing a research project on port cities. I was visiting a local seafarers' centre, asking about working conditions on the ships, which were reported to be unsafe and exploitative. The centre was in a run-down old building near the eastern port of Marseille, set up with different amenities – television, pool table, kitchen, bottles of perfume and newspapers – to cater for the needs of returning seafarers. It was staffed by retired French seafarers who liked to reminisce about maritime life. On the afternoon of my visit, a ship was about to dock, and I was invited to come along to greet the seafarers returning to land after months at sea.

Most of the cargo that enters Marseille arrives on giant container ships at the western port several miles outside the city, at Fos-sur-Mer, while the small eastern port close to the city centre accepts diverse cargo, such as dry bulk. Three seafarers stumbled out of the creaky ship, a look of thirst in their eyes. They came from Eastern Europe. To the disappointment of the retired seafarers back at the centre, they had no interest in talking about life on the sea, only in what goods were available – one bought a bottle of perfume – and in getting out into the city.

I like shipyards too, especially old ones. They are fraught with human striving. There is a romance to shipbuilding: the feats of science, engineering and craftsmanship, and the sense of collective endeavour, creating and setting forth vessels into the world. But there are dark sides to shipbuilding as well, contaminated with asbestos, built for empire and war.

In 2005, I visited Swan Hunter in Newcastle-upon-Tyne, 'the last shipyard on the Tyne', which was about to close its doors. I interviewed one of the few remaining shipbuilders at Swan Hunter for my research project, a shop steward who expressed anger over the destruction of the industry, blaming Margaret Thatcher. He reflected on the symbolic and economic importance of the shipyard, with a profound sense of loss, not only of jobs but of feeling valued, and asked, 'How can an island exist without ships?'[3]

After Swan Hunter closed, the Fairfield shipyard at Govan in Glasgow picked up its unfinished work, completing a dock landing ship for the Royal Fleet Auxiliary. Despite the decline of shipbuilding over the past century in Glasgow, they still build ships at the old Fairfield yard, warships equipped with state-of-the-art radar, weapons systems and propulsion.

The Fairfield Heritage shipbuilding museum is located ten minutes' walk west of Govan subway station, only three stops from the university, the first one south of the Clyde. It is located inside a long red sandstone building next to the entrance to an active shipyard, a unique contrast between the nineteenth and twenty-first centuries. Community volunteers, mostly retired shipbuilders who enjoy sharing stories about the ships, greet visitors and offer bespoke tours. They tell visitors proudly how the museum was created in 2014 in the restored former managers' offices of the shipyard, which had lain derelict for several years.

The museum's exhibition features several of the ships that were built at Fairfield. I was pleased to find a photo of the ship my great-grandmother sailed on, with the caption: 'The elegant Canadian Pacific liner *Empress of Russia* passing Clydebank to run trials early in 1913.'

For me, a sense of belonging in Glasgow requires pilgrimage to the abandoned shipyards, not just to the ones held in suspended animation. The loss of shipbuilding is vital to the spirit of the city. I have no direct connection to that history, but I believe that to inhabit a place fully is to recognize its landmarks, including its scars.

The site I wanted to visit most was the international asbestos memorial located across from the former John Brown shipyard at Clydebank, unveiled in 2015, which I had read about and found moving, the idea of a collective memorial to people who have died from toxic exposures.

One rainy morning, early in the New Year of the Dragon, I made the short train journey west to Clydebank. It was closer and simpler than I had imagined, but miles away in cognitive distance.

I could see the huge blue cantilever crane on the Clyde from the train, towering alone above the stripped docks, echoing the one near the Science Centre. From the train station, I followed the road down towards the riverside. There was a sense of dereliction in the streets, with several boarded-up shops, and a weary look among the few people who walked past.

At the junction by the main road next to the Clyde, I stopped to check the location of the memorial. I was standing right next to it. Five metal plinths stood on the pavement like tombstones, a bit taller than me, with mirrored surfaces, inscribed with the names of hundreds of people who died from asbestos-related illness. Many, possibly most, were shipbuilders. Across the concrete pavement was the dedication, written in block letters: 'FOR ALL THOSE KNOWN AND UNKNOWN'.

I lingered for a few moments of contemplation, then walked down to the water.

The former docks along the Clyde were bare and pocked, lined with rusted mooring bollards. Apart from a jogger, there was nobody around. The place was bereft, haunted by silences. Like the story of my great-grandmother's neglected grave, and the century between us. I yearned to find truths to fill these silences. But unfilled silence can be comforting sometimes, a form of reverence.

Gazing into the calm grey water, I imagined my great-grandmother's ship sailing past me, out to sea, and her spirit, no longer hungry, shimmering and bright.

26. Stargazing

The tree buds arrived, fuzzy green, white and yellow, and suddenly I realized that I had passed the test of a Glasgow winter. It would be a stretch to say that I avoided winter depression altogether, but the seasons of the city surprised me. I didn't expect to like the rain. Glasgow is one of the wettest cities in the UK, located in a 'lost temperate rainforest of Britain'.[1] After it rains, the air smells damp and earthy. Sandstone changes colour: red to rust; blonde to gold. Rare bog moss grows. Unlike the constant winter rain in Vancouver, home of living rainforests, Glasgow's rain follows its own rhythms: the wettest month is January, and the driest is April.[2] No wonder that the Gaelic word for Glasgow, *Glaschu*, means 'dear green place' or 'green hollow'.

We moved flats again, to a quieter place. The wind rustled softly through our chimney shaft.

On weekends, we visited family in the Hillfoots, our son's image of paradise, spotting barn owls by day and sheep grazing high in the heathery Ochil Hills.

Every few weeks, I met with my new climate friends. Our conversations felt restorative, energizing. They understood climate grief and anxiety as collective responses to an unbalanced system, and focused their efforts on practical 'actions', ranging from direct confrontations with fossil fuel companies to educational and solidarity campaigns.

Mostly, I was grateful for the excuse of moving to stay at home and rest. I found encouragement in the words of Vietnamese Zen master, poet and peace activist Thich Nhat Hanh, who wrote: 'An essential condition to hear the call of the Earth and respond to her is silence. If you don't have silence in yourself, you cannot hear her call: the call of life.'[3] From this insight comes strength and healing.

Thich Nhat Hanh practised a form of 'engaged Buddhism', which goes beyond individual journeys of self-realization: waking up to the beauties of the Earth, to heal ourselves, and waking up to the suffering of the world, to help others. 'Once there is seeing,' he said, 'there must be acting. Otherwise, what's the use of seeing?'[4]

Just before the school Easter holidays, I met one of my climate friends for coffee. 'I have an idea for an action,' she told me excitedly. I loved her proposals, which sounded almost like performance art, involving props, costumes, kayaks and banner drops, things that might wake people up. After our coffee, we parted ways, hoping to make our ferry crossings to the Isles through the storms, drawn by the call of the Earth.

Barren, desolate, exposed. These were the words that came to mind as we drove into the rugged moorlands of Coll, although I knew that the island was rich with life.

The Isle of Coll is a small Hebridean island four miles west of Mull, which has a 'dark sky community' designation from DarkSky International. It is thirteen miles long and three miles at its widest, with a population of around 150 people. Aside from stargazing, one of its main attractions, listed on the Visit Coll website, is that it is a place 'to do absolutely nothing'.[5]

'Do you think that we will be able to see the stars tonight?' our son asked hopefully, glancing at the shifting layers of clouds.

'Maybe,' my husband said, slowing the car over the bumps along the single-track road. 'Let's see. If not, we have the rest of the week.'

Our holiday cottage was on the west coast of the island, part of a small group of white stone crofters' houses set into the hills, with spectacular views over the Atlantic Ocean. Beyond the traditional dry-stone walls, half a dozen Highland cows idled in the sloping fields.

We were the first guests of the season. When we entered the cottage living room, we were greeted by a bucket of muddy water, an array of tools scattered over the floor and a mouldy half-cup of coffee.

The owner took a while to answer his phone. He was apologetic. It seemed that there had been a mix-up about the date of our arrival. It was Easter Sunday, and we would have to wait until the next morning for someone to come by. The farmer who looked after the cottage was busy at the community's Easter celebrations.

We ventured into the kitchen to unpack the food we had brought and prepare lunch. Above the sink was an 'important warning notice' that said: 'Recent investigation has identified that the water supply is at risk from bacterial contamination which could be harmful to health.'

As a precaution, we were instructed to boil water for drinking, brushing teeth and preparing food. The notice also advised to take care not to swallow water when showering or bathing.

Somehow, we had missed the visitor information about water supplies on Coll. As we soon learned, through a patchy mobile data connection, the village of Arinagour is the only place on Coll that is connected to a mains water supply. The rest of the island, more than half the population, relies on private sources, mostly from burns (streams), springs and boreholes, which are contaminated with heavy metals, high acidity, bacteria and parasites, including E. Coli and Giardia. Different elements interact to make it difficult, if not impossible, to remove health hazards from the water, even through boiling.[6]

It was a useful exercise in mindfulness, confronting my fears of toxic contamination. I wondered how local residents coped with the issue of unsafe water in their everyday lives. Many had to travel several times a week to access safe drinking water from the public tap in Arinagour.[7]

We packed a few sandwiches and snacks, and our last bottle of water, then headed out for a walk to the closest beach. The village was a short drive away, and we could collect more water later.

We walked for half an hour or so in the warm afternoon sun, along a narrow single-track road, past grass, grey rocks, a dead hare and a pond. The whole time we were walking, not a single car drove by. We crossed paths with one walker and one family of cyclists, nodding hellos.

'Ah,' our son said, 'it is so peaceful here. My thoughts have gone away.' He was the first to respond to the call of this place, and I was the last. I still carried my ghosts with me; they were part of me now. But we all responded to it, in time, and in our own ways.

It was funny how our son immediately loved this spare, treeless landscape, where the air smelled not only of sea, but of manure. He said it was his favourite place ever; and that was before we even looked into the night sky.

We followed a path through a farmer's field into tufty sand dunes covered in machair, a rare coastal grassland unique to the western coasts of Scotland and Ireland, with fertile soil from a combination of shells washed in from the sea, low-intensity seasonal grazing and high species diversity. Beyond the machair dunes was the turquoise ocean and a white sandy beach.

For hours, we sat on smooth volcanic rocks, dipping our toes in pools, watching the ocean froth. The Isle of Coll, together with other Hebridean islands, has some of the oldest rocks on Earth: its 'basement' rocks are made of Lewisian Gneiss, which are around 3 billion years old.

The machair dunes stood behind us, like soft furry creatures, buffering sound.

In the cottage, we found relics from other times. In the middle of the dining table, there was a bowl filled with pebbles and shells, and, disconcertingly, a small mammal's skull. The TV was the blocky kind from the 1980s, like the first one my parents had. We tried watching it, but it made such an unbearable hum we had to switch it off.

One of the window ledges in the living room was stacked with sun-bleached books, mainly travel guides and crime novels. I pulled out a book about the history of land use in Scotland, published in the 1990s, and read about the history of crofting, the tradition of small agricultural land holdings. I was surprised to learn that in crofting communities, cows – one of the largest agricultural contributors to greenhouse gas emissions – are seen as more sustainable than sheep, because they graze carefully, whereas sheep eat grass down to its roots.[8]

The chapter talked about the creation of crofting townships through the 1886 Crofters Holdings Act, which gave tenant farmers security over the land that they worked, a legacy of the previous century of land dispossession. In the mid-1700s, during the Highland Clearances, landowners evicted thousands of tenant farmers from the Scottish Highlands to make way for profitable sheep farms. Many displaced farmers and their families migrated to North America, Australia and the Scottish Lowlands. They followed other Highlanders who fled after the Jacobite Rebellion, when 'Bonnie Prince Charlie' of the House of Stewart attempted to take over the British throne with the support of Scottish Highlanders, resulting in a bloody defeat at the Battle of Culloden in 1746. Thousands of Highlanders died, either directly in battle or in the months of violent persecution that followed.[9]

My mom traces her family roots in Scotland to the 1700s, but to the Lowlands, not the Highlands, and I don't know when they migrated to Ireland, or what kinds of battles they fought.

Reading about crofting, I realized that in spite of cultural differences, my ancestors shared similar histories across Scotland, Ireland and South China: they all came from rural farming communities, who migrated to escape land conflicts. This is a shared history for a great many people, who abandoned old forms of knowledge about the land within the span of just a few generations. My husband's grandparents also came from farming families.

How could I connect with my ancestors, knowing so little about rural life? Yet in the gentle embrace of the machair dunes, which we returned to sit by every day, I felt supported.

The only night we saw the stars was our first. The rest were cloudy, as another storm gathered pace. As if by magic, the clouds of the day drifted back over the ocean, and the sky grew clear and dark. We set up our astronomy binoculars on a tripod behind the cottage and waited for twilight to fade. By ten o'clock, stars covered the sky, and we began.

We could see so many more stars than ever before: the Pleiades star cluster near the north star; the twin stars of Gemini. Our son loved seeing the Milky Way, visible with our naked eyes. My highlight was seeing the moons of Jupiter.

I kept waiting for the sky to get darker still, to experience the euphoria of a pure dark sky, when the eyes adjust to ever-deeper layers of the universe, revealing its ancient light. One of the houses nearby had its porch light on, which spoiled our night vision, and the horizon continued to glow. Full darkness probably wouldn't happen until after midnight, but by eleven o'clock, the clouds were starting to hem in, blotting out patches of sky. The next time would surely be better.

27. Qingming

This year, I wanted to celebrate Qingming somehow, instead of just marking the date. Qingming is like a spring cleaning of land and spirit relationships. Fields are ploughed and fertilized before sowing; ancestral graves are tidied.[1] I thought we could visit the two standing stones at the west end of Coll, known as *Na Sgeulachan*, which means 'teller of tales' in Gaelic. The precise archaeological origins of the stones are uncertain, possibly ancient burial markers, or the remains of a place of worship. I did not know what kind of offering I might make, but it seemed like a fitting place.

On our fourth day on Coll, two days before Qingming, we took the hour-long ferry to the Isle of Tiree for a day trip. Tiree is flatter and windier than Coll, a surfing destination in summer. Twelve miles long, three miles wide, a sister island.

We walked along an expanse of sandy beach. My husband and son flew a foil power kite, wrestling with the wind, while I paced, trying to stay warm, watching the terns. The only other people we saw were dog walkers, and another family flying a kite.

The fields and farmhouses across the road from the beach reminded me of the Canadian prairies. It was arresting, the juxtaposition of farm and sea.

After the beach, we went to find a place for lunch. We tried the main village of Scarinish, but the cafés were all closed. It was the off-season. My husband suggested a café in the Tiree Rural Centre, a ten-minute drive. On the way there, we passed several working farms. From the car, my son and I counted dozens of small birds in the grass with wispy black crests: lapwings, once a common farmland bird, now on the Red List of threatened species.[2]

The café was closed, but the rural centre was open. Information panels on the walls described Tiree's traditional crofting system, and its unique landscape of coastal machair, sliabh (rough inland peaty land) and in-bye (reclaimed crofters' land between machair and sliabh).

We went back to Scarinish, bought buns, cheese and crisps at the local Coop, and ate huddled together at a picnic table in the car park, buffeted by winds.

The next morning, in Coll, my husband got a text message from the ferry company. A major storm was approaching that weekend, and ferry cancellations were expected. We were advised to book onto a ferry the next morning: Qingming.

We were all disappointed to have to leave early, but we respected the power of gale force winds. The standing stones could wait.

That night, moths took refuge in our son's bedroom, nestling in gaps in the vaulted wood ceiling, and he could not sleep. The winds rocked the windowpanes through the night, and I stayed awake for a long time too.

On Qingming, we travelled all day and arrived home in Glasgow in the late afternoon. It was a relief to be back, with fresh tap water, and strangely clear skies. Outside our front window, a small cherry tree had suddenly blossomed in the park across the street, alone among the others, its pale pink flowers radiant in the sun. An offering.

Epilogue

It was a gift to find something left of my roots in my ancestral village, after nearly a century of dislocation. I have learned a lot from my hungry ghosts. They tell me that I do not need to sweep their tombs, any more than I need to build them a house. Their spirits dispersed into the karmic cycle long ago.

My ancestors are part of me; I am their continuation. What I owe to my ancestors, I owe to myself, and to future generations. It took a long journey to realize this, and I have yet to find what we owe. I still seek; we all do. We grow restless if we sit for too long.

Zen Buddhists say we need to accept our ancestors, including those we admire and those who did harm.[1] Karma means 'action'. Every action has consequences, which cannot be undone. Only through self-acceptance can we turn our anger into compassion, as a basis for positive action. Anger is connected to hatred, one of the poisons of the mind. Yet as each year breaks new heat records and unfathomable wars persist, I cannot help thinking that some anger, some unquelled flame, is necessary to defend our lands and ourselves.

There is burning inside and outside. Our inheritance is crackling. All the creatures in the forests, terrified, engulfed in fires and smoke, fleeing, shrieking, huddling, silenced. Is it any comfort to think that we become one with the universe again, thrown back into the cycle?

I have no rituals to offer, only the distant solace of stardust. I would like to sing a song, but I cannot hold a tune. There is a knot in my throat.

I keep coming back to material things, like talismans, bringing feelings of safety and protection. Their solidity gives the illusion of permanence; they will outlast our lives. Three-billion-year-old rocks, 300-million-year-old sandstone, books.

Impermanence offers a different kind of sustenance, sweeter because of its fleeting nature. Within a week of the first cherry blossoms across from our home in Glasgow, the whole city is in bloom. We could be in China, Japan or Vancouver. For two glorious weeks, the air bursts with fragrance, and children play among the petals in the grass.

Live music also has this ephemeral quality. At my son's choral concert, I cry at the swell of young voices, pleading for rain and peace, celebrating each other. Their voices, more than anything, bring me hope.

Between solidity and impermanence are the hills that surround us. They are not an escape but a home, calling us to return, again and again, to ourselves. Living mountains, as the Scottish poet Nan Shepherd calls them.[2] Sacred mountains, which are gaining legal rights as persons in many countries, alongside rivers and other ecosystems.[3] For Buddhists, mountains and forests are sites of pilgrimage and retreat, where you can reach Nirvana. They are not just locations to contain us, but places that are intrinsically part of us and our collective cycle.

Grandfather Mah closed his memoirs with a note of gratitude and reverence for his youth in the Rocky Mountains and the lyrics of the popular 1929 folk song, 'When It's Springtime in the Rockies'.[4] After spending most of his life in Ontario, he still felt, like his ancestors, that the Exalted Hills were his spiritual home.

From high points in Glasgow – the university's tower, the Necropolis – we can see hills in the distance, covered in wind turbines. Whitelee, the UK's largest onshore windfarm: here, there are emblems of a promised green future, yet already it feels post-apocalyptic. Hulking blades, like disembodied wings of a jet plane, whorl and clang. Looking up, we flinch as they appear to slice us. Across miles of rolling moorlands, there is a forest of metallic friends. Some stand still, resting, or defunct. Sheep, tagged blue, wander through meadows, devouring roots among tall thistles. Merlins hover and dive. The closest lookout is enclosed in a dry-stone-wall circle, with a gate to keep out the sheep. Northwest, we can see Glasgow and the Clyde valley; southwest, the Isle of Arran through fast-moving clouds, and its highest peak, Goatfell, another horizon.

In these Exalted Hills we connect to other hills, where we and our ancestors have travelled, distant but still held in our bodies. One, across time and place. I am not ready to retreat into the mountains just yet: we have fires to tend.

Acknowledgements

Thank you to the Mah clan and all my ancestors and relations. To my parents, sisters, brother and our extended families, I am grateful for your gifts of love, compassion and kindness.

To my editor, Casiana Ionita, thank you for your brilliant vision and edits, and for encouraging me to trust my intuition. Thanks to the Penguin team for your dedication to craft.

I am thankful to Loretta Lou, Wendy Chen, Xinhong Wang and Zhiling Ma for your invaluable research assistance and translation work. Thank you to the Toxic Expertise research team for your collaborations. Many thanks to Colin Stephen, Erica Mah and Alistair Fraser for your generous and perceptive comments on drafts.

I am grateful for the places that nourish us and for my travelling companions on this journey. To my cousin and her husband: thank you for coming with me to China. Thank you to my colleagues and students at the Universities of Warwick and Glasgow for our inspiring conversations. Thank you to my book club in Coventry; my friends in the climate and environmental justice movements; and friends across different places and phases of life, for your solidarity and shared understanding.

Deepest thanks and appreciation to my husband and son, who lived this book with me: you teach me about joy, infinite love and interconnection every day.

Note on Transliteration

My Chinese ancestors spoke Taishanese, a dialect of the Yue branch of Chinese, which includes Cantonese, Kaipingnese and several other dialects from different regions of Guangdong in South China. Due to the ad hoc ways that customs officials recorded the surnames and places of origin of early Chinese immigrants to Canada, there are multiple variants of transliteration (or romanization) in official records. For example, the villages in Taishan, which my grandfather described, have several variants, and some are known by different names today. For reasons of privacy, the villages in Taishan are given English pseudonyms. While some Chinese words and phrases in the book are drawn from my grandfather's memoirs, others use Mandarin pinyin romanization for ease of interpretation, such as the numbers for four (*si*) and eight (*ba*).

Notes

Prologue

1 The project was 'Toxic Expertise: Environmental Justice and the Global Petrochemical Industry', funded by the European Research Council (ERC) under the European Union's Horizon 2020 research and innovation programme (Grant Agreement No. 639583). Additional funding for research in China and British Columbia discussed in this book was provided by the Leverhulme Trust through the Philip Leverhulme Prize.

2 Henry Mah, *Memoirs of a Chinese Canadian*, unpublished family memoirs, written in the late 1980s.

3 Mah, *Memoirs of a Chinese Canadian*, 17–18. The memoir varies in the use of initial capitals for 'Mother' and 'Father'. For consistency, all quotes from the memoir use initial capitals.

4 Also Gim San, Gam Saan and other variants; 'Gim Shan' is the variant used in my grandfather's memoirs.

5 James Watson and Evelyn S. Rawski, eds., *Death Ritual in Late Imperial and Modern China*, University of California Press, 1988.

6 Mah, *Memoirs of a Chinese Canadian*, 18.

7 Watson and Rawski, eds., *Death Ritual in Late Imperial and Modern China*.

8 Costantino Moretti, 'The Thirty-Six Categories of "Hungry Ghosts" Described in the Sūtra of the Foundations of Mindfulness of the True Law', in Vincent Durand Dastès, ed., *Fantômes dans l'Extrême-Orient D'hier et D'aujourd'hui: Ghosts in the Far East in the Past and Present*, INALCO, 2017, 43–69.

Part I: Qingming

1. Western Peaceful Place

1 My grandfather used the Cantonese transliteration 'Toisan' and translation of 'Exalted Hills' in his memoirs, but this book uses the most common transliteration in pinyin, 'Taishan'.
2 Mah, *Memoirs of a Chinese Canadian*, 15.
3 Ibid., 17.
4 Ibid., 46.

2. Eastern Clan Village

1 Yang Su, *Collective Killings in Rural China During the Cultural Revolution*, Cambridge University Press, 2011, 37–8.
2 Ibid., 2.
3 Officially, *qiaopi* stopped in 1979 when they were incorporated into the Chinese Banking System, but the expectations of overseas money from returners continues. Shuhua Chen, 'De-labelling the "Memory of the World": A Cosmopolitan Perspective on Qiaopi Remittance Letters', *Anthropological Forum*, 2024.

4 Julia Lovell, *The Opium War*, Picador, 2012.

5 Madeline Y. Hsu, *Dreaming of Gold, Dreaming of Home: Transnationalism and Migration Between the United States and South China, 1882–1943*, Stanford University Press, 2000.

6 Ibid.

7 William Poy Lee, *The Eighth Promise: An American Son's Tribute to His Toisanese Mother*, Rodale Press, 2007.

3. Hot Springs Hotel

1 Gang Song, Boyou Zhang, Xinming Wang, Jingping Gong, Daniel Chan, John Bernett and S. C. Lee, 'Indoor Radon Levels in Selected Hot Spring Hotels in Guangdong, China', *Science of the Total Environment* 339(1–3) (2005): 63–70.

2 Yuanni Wang and Loretta Lou, 'Can a Hot Spring Resort Coexist with a Chemical Industry Park? The Case of Jiangsu, China', *Toxic News*, 17 November 2020.

6. The Gifts

1 Jonathan Hammond, 'Ecological and Cultural Anatomy of Taishan Villages', *Modern Asian Studies* 29(3) (1995): 569.

2 Feng Zhang, 'Remittances, Donations, and Investments in Taishan, China, Since 1978: A Transnational Development Pattern', PhD dissertation, University of British Columbia, 2007; Ellen Oxfeld, 'Imaginary Homecomings: Chinese Villagers, Their Overseas Relations, and Social Capital', *The Journal of Socio-Economics* 30(2) (2001): 181–6.

3 Edward Wong, 'Fortresses Inspired by West Crumble in a New China', *The New York Times*, 3 December 2009; Nicholas D. Kristof, 'Taishan Journal; The Wellspring of Chinatowns Still Bubbles Over', *The New York Times*, 7 November 1987; Oxfeld, 'Imaginary Homecomings'.

4 Chen, 'De-labelling the "Memory of the World"'.

5 Gregor Benton and Hong Liu, 'Qiaopi (僑批) and Charity', in John Fitzgerald and Hon-ming Yip, eds., *Chinese Diaspora Charity and the Cantonese Pacific, 1850–1949*, Oxford University Press, 2020, 51–71.

7. The House

1 Mah, *Memoirs of a Chinese Canadian*, 17.

9. The Neglected Grave

1 Steve A. Smith, 'Talking Toads and Chinless Ghosts: The Politics of "Superstitious" Rumors in the People's Republic of China, 1961–1965', *The American Historical Review* 111(2) (2006): 405–27.

2 Li Meng and Yang Liao, 'The Changes of Clan, Ancestral Hall and Management in Urban-Village Community: A Case of Investigation-based on Village *Changban*, Guangzhou, China', *Journal of Research in Humanities and Social Science* 9(3) (2021): 32–43.

Part II: Hungry Ghosts

10. Pollution

1 Woo (alternatively Hu, Wu, Wou, You, Yu et al.) is a Cantonese transliteration of several different Chinese surnames, each with different meanings. My grandfather included the handwritten Chinese character (胡) for his mother's clan name in his memoirs, which enabled me to identify the correct translation. See: My China Roots, 'Woo Chinese Last Name Facts', https://www.mychin-aroots.com/surnames

2 Mah, *Memoirs of a Chinese Canadian*, 1.

3 Myron Cohen, 'Souls and Salvation: Conflicting Themes in Chinese Popular Religion', in Watson and Rawski, eds., *Death Ritual in Late Imperial and Modern China*, 180–202.

4 Moretti, 'The Thirty-Six Categories of "Hungry Ghosts"', 44.

5 Approximately 98–99 per cent of petrochemicals are derived from fossil fuels, including oil, gas and coal, and the remaining 1–2 per cent come from sugar and other bio-based materials. The largest market for petrochemicals is plastics (80 per cent), but petrochemicals are also used for several other synthetic products, such as fertilizers, paints, solvents and rubbers. Every stage of the oil-to-plastics lifecycle, from extraction to refining, to consumption and waste, poses significant environmental health hazards. For an overview of the study, see Alice Mah, *Petrochemical Planet: Multiscalar Battles of Industrial Transformation*, Duke University Press, 2023.

6 Emily Martin, 'Gender and Ideological Differences in Representations of Life and Death', in Watson and Rawski, eds., *Death Ritual in Late Imperial and Modern China*, 164–79.

7 Chris Buckley, 'Rice Tainted with Cadmium is Discovered in Southern China', *The New York Times*, 21 May 2023; Shen Ke, Xi-Yu Cheng, Ni Zhang, Hong-Gang Hu, Qiong Yan, Ling-Ling Hou, Xin Sun and Zhi-Nan Chen, 'Cadmium Contamination of Rice from Various Polluted Areas of China and its Potential Risks to Human Health', *Environmental Monitoring and Assessment* 187 (2015): 1–11; Yuanan Hu, Hefa Cheng and Shu Tao, 'The Challenges and Solutions for Cadmium-Contaminated Rice in China: A Critical Review', *Environment International* 92 (2016): 515–32.

11. Illness

1 Daniel L. Sudakin, David L. Stone and Laura Power, 'Naphthalene Mothballs: Emerging and Recurring Issues and Their Relevance to Environmental Health', *Current Topics in Toxicology* 7 (2011): 13; Divyanshu Dubey, Vibhash D. Sharma, Steven E. Pass, Anshudha Sawhney and Olaf Stüve, 'Para-dichlorobenzene Toxicity: A Review of Potential Neurotoxic Manifestations', *Therapeutic Advances in Neurological Disorders* 7(3) (2014): 177–87.

2 Mah, *Memoirs of a Chinese Canadian*, 4.

3 Ibid., 1.

4 The ship record was retrieved from the digital database *Immigrants from China 1885–1959*, Library and Archives, Canada. Reference: RG 76 D2a, Volume 1066.

5 Mah, *Memoirs of a Chinese Canadian*, 9.

6 Ibid., 24–5.

7 At a high school in Taishan funded by overseas money, Amanda and Lily found a plaque noting this fact during their first trip to the Mah village in 2017.

8 Ibid., 77.

9 Ibid., 102–3.

10 Ibid., 108–9.

11 In addition to the school climate strikes, one of the key reasons for the rising global public concern about the climate emergency in 2019 was the publication of the IPCC Report 'Global Warming of 1.5 °C' in 2018, warning that humanity needs to cut greenhouse emissions in half by 2030 and reach 'net zero' carbon emissions by 2050, or else face untold catastrophe. Valérie Masson-Delmotte, Panmao Zhai, Hans-Otto Pörtner, Debra Roberts, Jim Skea, Priyadarshi R. Shukla, Anna Pirani et al., *Global Warming of 1.5°C: An IPCC Special Report*, Intergovernmental Panel on Climate Change, 2018.

12 Timothy M. Lenton et al., 'Climate tipping points – too risky to bet against', *Nature* 575(7784) (2019): 592–5; David Wallace-Wells, *The Uninhabitable Earth: A Story of the Future*, Penguin UK, 2019.

13 Lisa A. Hamilton, Steven Feit, Carroll Muffett et al., *Plastic and Climate: The Hidden Costs of a Plastic Planet*, Center for International Environmental Law, 2019; Peter Stoett and Joanna Vince, 'The Plastic–Climate Nexus', in Paul G. Harris, ed., *Climate Change and Ocean Governance: Politics and Policy for Threatened Seas*, Cambridge University Press, 2019, 345–61.

14 Alice Mah, *Plastic Unlimited: How Corporations are Fuelling the Ecological Crisis and What We Can Do About It*, Polity Press, 2022.

15 International Renewable Energy Agency, *Reaching Net Zero With Renewables* (2020), https://www.irena.org/publications/2020/Sep/Reaching-Zero-with-Renewables

16 International Energy Agency, *The Future of Petrochemicals* (2018), https://www.iea.org/reports/ the-future-of-petrochemicals

12. Ravening

1 Mah, *Memoirs of a Chinese Canadian*, 5–6.

2 This handwritten letter is separate from my grandfather's memoirs, part of my family's miscellaneous home archive of family letters and papers.

3 This detail is also noted in my grandfather's letter, rather than in his memoirs. Clan records going back hundreds and even thousands of years throughout ancestral villages in China are recorded in Chinese clan genealogical books, known as *zupu* (族谱) or *jiapu* (家谱). See: My China Roots, 'Zupu', https://www.mychinaroots.com/wiki/article/zupu

4 Martin, 'Gender and Ideological Differences in Representations of Life and Death', 170; C. Fred Blake, 'Death and Abuse in Marriage Laments: The curse of Chinese brides', *Asian Folklore Studies* (1978): 13–33.

5 In an essay called 'Why am I a heathen?' written in 1887 by Wong Chin Foo, who was sponsored to come to the US from Canada by Christian missionaries, Wong contrasted the virtues of Confucian morality with the hypocrisy of

Christianity. He condemned Christian boasts about charitable acts and objected to the 'preposterous' Christian idea that sinners could commit terrible crimes yet be redeemed in the eleventh hour. Wong Chin Foo, 'Why Am I a Heathen?', *The North American Review* 145 (369) (1887): 169–79.

13. Climate Breakdown

1 Holmes Welch, *The Practice of Chinese Buddhism, 1900–1950*, Harvard University Press, 1967; Sheng Wenqiang, 'The Hungry Dead and the Envoys of Hell: China's Ghost Festival', Sixth Tone, 30 August 2023, https://www.sixthtone.com/news/1013627

2 Libby Brooks, 'Hundreds of global civil society representatives walk out of COP26 in protest', *The Guardian*, 12 November 2021.

3 John J. Clague, 'How an "atmospheric river" drenched British Columbia and led to floods and mudslides', *The Conversation*, 17 November 2021; Rhianna Schmunk, 'Thousands of animals have died on flooded B.C. farms in "agricultural disaster"', *CBC News*, 18 November 2021.

4 Cole Burston and Leyland Cecco, '"There's nothing left in Lytton": the Canadian village destroyed by wildfire – a picture essay', *The Guardian*, 25 July 2021; Vjosa Isai, 'Heat wave spread fire that "erased" Canadian town', *The New York Times*, 10 July 2021.

5 Cory Correia, 'Chinese history museum featuring 1,600 artifacts destroyed in Lytton wildfire', CBC News, 5 July 2021.

6 Emily Chung, 'Why are BC's floods so bad? Blame the wildfires', *CBC News*, 18 November 2021; Ian Austen and Vjosa Isai, 'Vancouver is marooned by flooding and besieged again by climate change', *The New York Times*, 21 November 2021.

7 Elizabeth McSheffrey, 'Sumas First Nation chief reflects on "disaster" B.C. flooding where lake used to be', *Global News*, 18 November 2021; 'The 100-year-old decision that contributed to Abbotsford, B.C., flooding', *CBC News*, 18 November 2021.

8 Robert Lynn Shervill, *Smithers: From Swamp to Village*, Town of Smithers, 1981. For an alternative account of the history of the town, see: Tyler McCreary, *Shared Histories: Witsuwit'en-Settler Relations in Smithers, British Columbia 1913–1973*, Creekstone Press, 2018.

9 Faye Chambers, 'Tracing the hidden River Sherbourne under Coventry', *BBC News*, 10 January 2015.

14. Inferno

1 In late Imperial and modern China, women sometimes used suicide as an act of aggression against their relatives in the 'desperate years after marriage when they are still under the thumb of mother-in-law'. Martin, 'Gender and Ideological Differences in Representations of Life and Death', 177.

2 Poon Shuk Wah, 'Refashioning Festivals in Republican Guangzhou', *Modern China* 30(2)(2004): 199–227.

3 Holy Isle, 'Wildlife on the Island', https://www.holyisle.org/the-island/wildlife-on-the-island

4 Myron Cohen, 'Souls and Salvation: Conflicting Themes in Chinese Popular Religion', in Watson and Rawski, eds., *Death Ritual in Late Imperial and Modern China*, 180–202.

16. Bones of Gold Mountain

1 Gabor Maté, *When the Body Says No: The Cost of Hidden Stress*, Vintage Canada, 2011.
2 My China Roots, 'Ma Surname Origins', https://www.mychinaroots.com/surnames
3 Government of Canada, 'Prime Minister Harper Offers Full Apology for the Chinese Head Tax', 22 June 2006, https://www.canada.ca/en/news/archive/2006/06/prime-minister-harper-offers-full-apology-chinese-head-tax.html
4 Mah, *Memoirs of a Chinese Canadian*, 3.
5 In the first half of the twentieth century, some 100,000 sets of bones made return journeys to China, via Hong Kong, from former Gold Rush Chinese communities in California, Canada and Australia. See: Alex Frew McMillan, 'Learning Lessons from the Grave: The remains of Chinese emigrants produced a paper trail of the modern Chinese world', The Chinese University of Hong Kong (CUHK), *Scholarly Updates*, August 2015.
6 *The Cranbrook Herald*, 'Chinese Example of Patriotism', Volume 17, no. 42, 21 October 1915.
7 *Hot Spring News*, 'Knights Against Chinese', 12 January 1892.
8 *The Cranbrook Herald*, 'Cranbrook Chinese Celebrate', 29 February 1912.
9 Ibid.

10 Mah, *Memoirs of a Chinese Canadian*, 11. Opium was only made illegal in Canada in 1908. There were frequent opium raids in Cranbrook's Chinatown. See: Jim Cameron, 'Chinatown: Janus Feature on the History of Cranbrook's Chinese Community Continues', Janus, *The Cranbrook Herald*, 12 March 2015.

11 Mah, *Memoirs of a Chinese Canadian*, 32.

12 Ibid.

13 Ibid., 30.

14 Gabor Maté, *In the Realm of Hungry Ghosts: Close Encounters with Addiction*, Random House Digital, Inc., 2008.

15 Ibid.

16 Maté, *When the Body Says No*.

17. Rituals

1 Watson and Rawski, eds., *Death Ritual in Late Imperial and Modern China*; Nicolas Standaert, *The Interweaving of Rituals: Funerals in the Cultural Exchange between China and Europe*, University of Washington Press, 2008; Sue Fawn Chung et al., eds., *Chinese American Death Rituals: Respecting the Ancestors*, AltaMira Press, 2005.

2 Steve Roud, *The Penguin Guide to the Superstitions of Britain and Ireland*, Penguin UK, 2006.

3 Alessandra Colaianni, 'Omens: Even surgeons can be superstitious', *Virginia Quarterly Review*, spring/summer 2023; Charlotte R. Brookfield, Patrick P.J. Phillips and Robert J. Shorten, 'Q fever – the superstition of avoiding the word "quiet" as a coping mechanism: randomised controlled non-inferiority trial', *BMJ* 367 (2019); Sukhpreet

Singh Dubb, A. Ferro and C. Fowell, '"Shh – don't say the Q-word" or do you?', *British Journal of Oral and Maxillofacial Surgery* 59(1) (2021): e13–e16.

4 Kat Huang, 'Study shows shared ancestor 800 years ago', *Yale News*, 8 October 2004.

5 Scott Hershberger, 'Humans are more closely related than we think', *Scientific American*, 5 October 2020.

Part III: Burnt Offerings

19. Incalculable Debts

1 In the early history of Gold Mountain, clan associations played a major role in supporting new overseas Chinese immigrants. To this day, the Mah Society remains one of the most significant historic clan associations in Canada, with headquarters in several cities, including the dilapidated five-storey Mah Society Association building in Vancouver's Chinatown.

20. A Buddhist Path

1 Walpola Sri Rahula, *What the Buddha Taught*, Oneworld, 2001, 68.

2 David Kortava, 'Lost in Thought: The Psychological Risks of Meditation', *Harpers Magazine*, April 2021; 'Untold: The Retreat – An Investigative Podcast into the Perils of Meditation', *Financial Times*, 2023.

3 Otto Simonsson and Simon B. Goldberg, 'Linkages Between Psychedelics and Meditation in a Population-based

Sample in the United States', *Journal of Psychoactive Drugs* 55, no. 1 (2023): 11–18.

4 Welch, *The Practice of Chinese Buddhism*; see also: Wenqiang, 'The Hungry Dead and the Envoys of Hell'.

21. Dirty Oil Road

1 Ruth Ozeki, Zen Buddhist monk and novelist, describes this practice in her novel *A Tale for the Time Being*, Viking, 2013; see also Zen master Thich Nhat Hanh's reflection on 'the joy of having toilets' in his book *At Home in the World*, Penguin, 2016.

2 https://coastal.climatecentral.org/

3 Author's interview with environmental activist, Grangemouth, 3 April 2019.

4 A pseudonym, in accordance with ethical guidelines of the British Sociological Association.

5 Author's interview with environmental activist, Grangemouth, 3 April 2019.

6 Lorenzo Feltrin, Alice Mah and David Brown, 'Noxious Deindustrialization: Experiences of Precarity and Pollution in Scotland's Petrochemical Capital', *Environment and Planning C: Politics and Space* 40(3) (2022): 950–69.

7 See Mah, *Petrochemical Planet*, 133–4.

8 Feltrin, Mah and Brown, 'Noxious Deindustrialization'.

9 Focus group interview, Grangemouth, 21 October 2019. Complaints of noise, light, and air pollution are common for many people who live in close proximity to the petrochemical industry, in countries all over the world, and it is not unique to INEOS. Complaints occur even in the case

where regulations are in place. Residents have numbers to call both to companies and to environmental agencies to report pollution incidents and accidents. Other residents in the focus group interviews in Grangemouth made complaints about the various effects of local pollution, as documented in Feltrin, Mah, and Brown. "Noxious Deindustrialization." The study was focused on reported experiences, not on measurements, of pollution. A parallel study in Fawley, Southampton, UK, found similar complaints among residents but higher levels of local acceptance of industry: Brown, David, Alice Mah, and Gordon Walker. "The Tenacity of Trust in Petrochemical Communities: Reckoning with Risk on the Fawley Waterside (1997–2019)." *Environment and Planning E: Nature and Space* 5, no. 3 (2022): 1207-1229.

10 Alice Mah, 'The Dereliction Tourist: Ethical Issues of Conducting Research in Areas of Industrial Ruination', *Sociological Research Online* 19(4) (2014): 162–75. My research focused on communities living in different areas of industrial ruination: derelict chemical factories in the North American Rust Belt; former shipyards in Northeast England; and abandoned textile factories in Western Russia.

11 https://coastal.climatecentral.org/

12 Jenness Mitchell, 'Grangemouth's "essential" flood defence cost could soar to £650m', *BBC News*, 21 January 2022.

13 The storyteller's name is Luke Winter, a writer who has published many 'stories for strangers' in collections, and writes on his website: 'Hi, I'm Luke. I write stories on the street for people like you, who walk by, see my typewriter and me, and smile.' https://www.storiesforstrangers.com/

22. Foraging

1 Ernest W. Burgess, 'The Growth of the City: An Introduction to a Research Project', in *The City Reader*, Routledge, 2015 (original 1925), 212–20.
2 Mah, *Memoirs of a Chinese Canadian*, 3.
3 Ibid., 8.
4 Ibid., 34.

23. Sound

1 Selected texts from the *Tipitaka*, in Rahula, *What the Buddha Taught*, 99.
2 Clayton Page Aldern, *The Weight of Nature: How a Changing Climate Changes our Brains, Minds and Bodies*, Penguin, 2024, 215.
3 Jesús Jiménez-Ruiz, Laurent Hardion, Juan Pablo Del Monte, Bruno Vila and M. Inés Santín-Montanyá, 'Monographs on Invasive Plants in Europe N° 4: *Arundo donax* L.', *Botany Letters* 168(1) (2021): 131–51; Gretchen C. Coffman, Richard F. Ambrose and Philip W. Rundel, 'Wildfire promotes dominance of invasive giant reed (*Arundo donax*) in riparian ecosystems', *Biological Invasions* 12 (2010): 2723–4.

24. Light

1 Bernardo Kastrup, *Science Ideated: The Fall of Matter and the Contours of the Next Mainstream Scientific Worldview*, John Hunt Publishing, 2021.

2 Ying-shih Yu, 'Oh Soul, Come Back: A Study of the Changing Conceptions of the Soul and Afterlife in Pre-Buddhist China', *Harvard Journal of Asiatic Studies* 47 (1987): 363–95; Steven Harrel, 'The Concept of Soul in Chinese Folk Religion', *Journal of Asian Studies* (1979): 519–28; James Watson, 'The Structure of Chinese Funerary Rites', in Watson and Rawski, eds., *Death Ritual in Late Imperial and Modern China*, 3–19.

3 Selected texts from the *Tipitaka*, in Rahula, *What the Buddha Taught*, 101–2.

25. Shipyards

1 *Immigrants from China 1885–1959*, Library and Archives, Canada. Reference: RG 76 D2a, Volume 1066.

2 Ibid.

3 Interview with shipbuilder, Swan Hunter, Newcastle-upon-Tyne, 2 December 2005.

26. Stargazing

1 It rains almost twice as much in Glasgow (137cm per year) as it does in Edinburgh (73cm per year); see: UK Met Office, UK Climate Averages, https://www.metoffice.gov.uk/research/climate/maps-and-data/uk-climate-averages; Guy Shrubsole, *The Lost Rainforests of Britain*, William Collins, 2023.

2 UK Met Office, UK Climate Averages, https://www.metoffice.gov.uk/research/climate/maps-and-data/uk-climate-averages

3 Thich Nhat Hanh, *Zen and the Art of Saving the Planet*, Penguin, 2021, 1–2.

4 Ibid., v.

5 Visit Coll, Attractions – Nothing, https://visitcoll.co.uk/nothing

6 Visit Coll, Utilities – Water supplies on Coll, https://visitcoll.co.uk/water

7 Rita Campbell, 'Residents forced to travel six miles for drinking water on Hebridean island', *Press and Journal*, 15 December 2020.

8 Donald Mackay, *Scotland's Rural Land Use Agencies*, Scottish Cultural Press, 1995.

9 Ibid.; see also: Eric Richards, *Debating the Highland Clearances*, Edinburgh University Press, 2007.

27. Qingming

1 Göran Aijmer, 'Ancestors in the Spring: The Qingming Festival in Central China', *Journal of the Hong Kong Branch of the Royal Asiatic Society* (1978): 59–82.

2 RSBP, Lapwing, https://www.rspb.org.uk/birds-and-wildlife/lapwing

Epilogue

1 Thich Nhat Hanh, *Fear*, Penguin, 2012.

2 Nan Shepherd, *The Living Mountain: A Celebration of the Cairngorm Mountains of Scotland*, Canongate Books, 2008.

3 Gwendolyn J. Gordon, 'Environmental Personhood', *Colum. J. Envtl. L.* 43 (2018): 49; Christopher D. Stone,

'Should Trees Have Standing? – Toward Legal Rights for Natural Objects', *Southern California Law Review* 45 (1972): 450–501.

4 Mary Hale Woolsey, 1929, cited in Mah, *Memoirs of a Chinese Canadian*, 130–31.